Praise for *Maki*

"In a hyper-competitive and complex world, it's not enough to meet expectations and be "good" at what you do. In order to stand out, inspire and lead exceptional teams and organizations, you have to be remarkable. Remarkable leaders are ethical, catalytic, and transparent, and apply the right strategies across their entire enterprise. Only then will you deliver the highest value to all your organization's stakeholders. Adam Legge wrote the book that walks readers from basic tenets, to common challenges leaders face, through practical application of remarkable thinking and strategy within your organization. This isn't a book about leadership style. It's a road map, workbook and your go-to leadership doctrine all rolled into one."

- Sheree Anne Kelly, President & CEO, Association of Chamber of Commerce Executives

"I wish I would have had a step-by-step process to become remarkable when I accepted my first CEO position. Many of the lessons I learned the hard way are included in *Making Remarkable*."

- Tim Giuliani, President and CEO, Orlando Economic Partnership

"Adam's approach motivates and inspires you to challenge the status quo, to think and act boldly. *Making Remarkable* provides a purposeful roadmap for leaders to transform organizations and cultures to deliver impactful results."

- Mark Eagan CCE, CEO, Capital Region Chamber, Albany, NY

"Making Remarkable provides an easy to follow roadmap to remarkability. It is well written and provides great insights, direction and tools for organizational leadership. It is both inspirational and informative. Author, Adam Legge is a great storyteller who gives a poignant personal perspective and also knowledge gained from other experts. While geared to beginning your leadership journey, I found great nuggets that apply to an experienced CEO. I would highly recommend to anyone running or considering running an organization."
  - Betty Nokes Capestany, President & CEO, Bellevue Chamber of Commerce

"Adam Legge shows you both sides of organizational management: the top of the leadership mountain and the underbelly of change."
  - Kyle Sexton, ChamberThink Strategies
    Author of *Remembership* and *Follow You Anywhere*

"I have had the opportunity to serve with Adam Legge on both the Association of Chamber of Commerce Executives Board and World Chamber Federation General Council. He is without a doubt a global thought leader in the Chamber of Commerce industry. *Making Remarkable* is an excellent "how to" resource for both new and seasoned Chamber CEOs on modernizing your organization to achieve better results, more satisfied members, and more engaged staff."
  - Jay Byers, CEO, Greater Des Moines Partnership

"As the pace of change accelerates, organizations are seeking ways to stay ahead of—not just respond to—change. Adam's book is part case study, part textbook, and all inspiration. It

gives evidence-based advice about how to recognize an organization's need for transformation and how to get there."
- Jennifer Diakiw, President, Ernest C. Manning Awards Foundation

"What I would've given 25 years ago as a new CEO to have had the benefit of *Making Remarkable*. Nowhere else have I seen such a comprehensive, yet targeted, resource to molding a remarkable organization with a continuous eye towards truly being a differentiator. Adam Legge provides real world examples as well as personal insight into what today's organizations are looking for in their leaders. Beyond that, it is also a valuable reminder to those who have long been in leadership roles where they are in their remarkable journey!"
- Jay Chesshir, President and CEO, Little Rock Regional Chamber & 2017/18 ACCE Board Chair

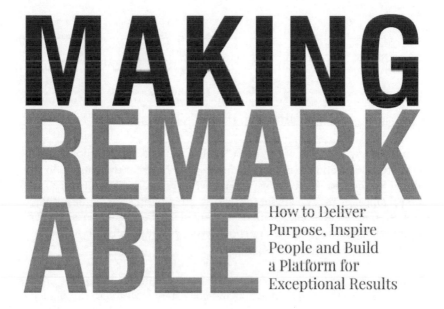

MAKING
REMARK
ABLE

How to Deliver
Purpose, Inspire
People and Build
a Platform for
Exceptional Results

ADAM LEGGE

www.makingremarkable.com

Cover design: Sara Swallow
Interior: BlitzPrint

Making Remarkable/Adam W. Legge. – 1st ed.
Print   ISBN 978-1-7753927-0-5
e-book   ISBN 978-1-7753927-1-2

This book is dedicated to every leader who has a permanent dissatisfaction with the status quo.

And to my children—it is for them I wish to leave this place a little better than I found it.

"It is the time to dare and endure."

Winston S. Churchill
1940

Foreword

The not-for-profit model is mature at best. It is struggling to perform in an environment it wasn't designed for. Time pressures, higher member expectations, generational value differences, increased competition, and rapidly emerging (and often disruptive) technologies have converged to create an unfriendly landscape. As a result, many not-for-profits are struggling, and some are in unquestionable decline.

In 1965, the American Medical Association membership represented 75% of U.S. physicians. Today that share is 17%. The Boy Scouts membership dropped from 4.6 million in 1995 to 2.3 million in 2017. Membership in the Masons has declined from 4 million in 1950 to under 1 million today. The Jaycees peaked at 356,000 in 1976 and now have under 10,000 members.

The imperative is clear: innovate. Think differently. Shake off the past and try the new.

Since the release of *Race for Relevance, Five Radical Changes for Associations* in 2011, non-profit volunteer leaders and staff have recognized the need for change. Associations have addressed their governance structures and processes, eliminating unproductive bureaucracies and emphasizing appropriate board composition. And non-profits have endeavored to improve their focus on where they have unique value in an increasingly competitive environment. A few have achieved remarkable transformations while others have struggled to effect meaningful change.

What have we learned from those who have succeeded?

First, change starts at the top. You have to take your governance seriously. Attracting the competencies on your board that are aligned with the organization's opportunities and challenges is critical. And size does matter. Large, unwieldy boards simply don't produce. And this should be no surprise – the research on the superior effectiveness of small teams is overwhelming.

Next, you won't get far without a sense of urgency. The clock is ticking. Every day that you tolerate the status quo makes it more difficult to change course. And non-profit leaders have learned that data can be a powerful tool in creating that sense of urgency.

They understand that trying to do too much, while noble, is seriously flawed. Members are not fooled by long lists of marginal programs, services and products. And spreading scarce resources across a bloated product line is simply mismanagement.

Finally, collegiality can kill you. The unwillingness to challenge colleagues, the acceptance of subpar performance from directors and the reluctance to ruffle the feathers of peers all corrupt the change process. If you are not careful, the proponents for the status quo will water down any attempts to transform the organization.

Not-for-profit leaders and staff are cautious. Their organizations have strong traditions that resist change. Everyone wants to know "Who has done it?" "Tell me about another non-profit that made radical changes and the organization's performance improved as a result." I get this question constantly.

So, here is one. Adam Legge did it. He took an organization from the edge of irrelevance to one that is remarkable. He provides hands-on insights into what works and what doesn't. Not what a consultant thinks will work. Not a professor's theories. But from a CEO who took to the challenges and passionately effected change.

In *Making Remarkable: How to Deliver Purpose, Inspire People and Build a Platform for Exceptional Results*, Adam provides a straight-forward framework and actions that address the challenges I identified above so that your organization doesn't join the ranks of the irrelevant. Whether it is dealing with governance changes or optimizing resources and competitive position by abandoning obsolete or unproductive programs, he has done it and shares with you his experience and valuable insights. I am confident that if you put these ideas and practices to work in your organization, you will realize greater relevance, improved value and increased member engagement.

Harrison Coerver
Co-author of *Race for Relevance, Five Radical Changes for Associations*
May 2018

CHAPTER 1: Introduction

The Back Story

In 2010, I was comfortable in my role as the vice president of my city's economic development agency. So, when I was approached by a headhunter asking if I would consider putting my hat in the ring for the position of President and CEO of the Calgary Chamber of Commerce, my first reaction was to decline it.

"The Chamber of Commerce?" I thought to myself. "That stuffy old place? The one in the building that time forgot? Why would I want to lead that organization?"

The more I spoke to the headhunter, however, the more intrigued I became. It was an opportunity to lead. To change something. To make something better. To leave my mark. A chance to develop a skill set that would be transferable to other jobs, roles and organizations throughout my career.

I said yes.

I'll be honest: I didn't know where to start. The challenges that the Chamber was facing were significant: financial difficulties, disengaged staff, declining membership and support, struggles adapting to the changing world, legacy staffing issues, a weak brand and a relatively non-existent value proposition.

The early days were hard; I spent those first weeks and months digging into the situation—meeting people, looking at numbers, assessing and being curious. I talked to a lot of people. I read a lot of books and resources and listened to a lot of TED talks and

1

podcasts on transformation, innovation and great organizations.

What I really needed was a resource, guide or plan to help me to plan and execute this massive organizational transformation.

It didn't exist.

One night, about six months in, I came home and confessed to my wife: "I think I made a huge mistake taking this job. There's so much to fix. I want this place to be remarkable, but I don't know how to get it there."

She thought for a moment, and supportively said, "Well, I guess you better come up with a plan and get to it, then."

This book is that plan.

What is Remarkability?

In my 20 years of leadership, I have found that when you ask leaders about their ultimate objective, they all say things like "to transform the organization," "to increase its relevance and impact," or "to make a difference." All these things are outcomes of a greater state—organizational remarkability. What all these leaders really want to achieve is *remarkability*.

Making Remarkable was written for leaders who want to make their organization remarkable.

What is remarkability? It is a state of being exceptional in your performance, relevance and value. It is being in a state that enables your organization to do its finest work and to therefore make an unparalleled impact on your customers, members, communities and the world.

Remarkability has three pillars—Purpose, People, and Platform—each of which I will discuss in detail. I will also identify the condition or state that each of these pillars needs to be at if you are to achieve remarkability, and what you will need to do to get from where you are to remarkable.

Why remarkable? Remarkable enables the finest work to be done. Remarkable makes the biggest impact and leaves the greatest legacy. People pay attention to remarkable. Remarkable gets the best people. Remarkable gets the best funding. Remarkable is a magnet. Remarkable is irresistible.

No one wants average, mediocre or struggling. People want remarkable.

What are the benefits of transforming into a remarkable organization? Greater impact. Better revenues and growth. Increased relevance. Legacy. Better staff retention and recruitment. Greater engagement. More satisfied customers and members. Bigger fans. Enhanced profile and reputation. Improved morale and more high-fives around the office.

The Never-Ending Journey

The journey to remarkability is not a one-and-done proposition. *Making Remarkable* outlines a process for transforming into a remarkable organization, but you should not view this as a "start and finish" kind of process. There is no "done." You can't "set and forget."

Making an organization remarkable requires a constant state of surveying, adapting, measuring and repeating. The scale, pace and magnitude of change in the world is so great that it is nearly impossible to sit back and revel in your remarkable awesomeness. A great leader will get to a place of remarkability and create a culture that continually assesses its world and looks to evolve and adapt. Every being must adapt to its surroundings or it will wither. Organizations are no different. One of my favourite quotes, and a personal life mantra, comes from Darren Entwistle, the CEO of TELUS, one of Canada's largest telecommunications companies: "I have a permanent dissatisfaction with the status quo." Leaders of remarkable organizations need to have a healthy, yet constant, dissatisfaction with the status quo.

Why *Making Remarkable*?

I wrote *Making Remarkable* because, when I was trying to find my footing as a new leader, there were no comprehensive resources to help me or to mark out the path to making my organization remarkable.

Making Remarkable is for those who have accepted the call of leadership, potentially for the first time. It is for those who have been tasked with making their organization extraordinary through change and transformation. It is for those who want their organization to rise above the masses and achieve remarkable things. It is meant for leaders who believe that their organization is capable of doing greater things but aren't sure how to enable it to do so.

Making Remarkable is meant to be a helpful guide along an uncertain, winding, challenging, but rewarding path. It is the guide and the plan that I wish I'd had when I took on the challenge at the Calgary Chamber. It is meant to help make sense of uncertainty and complexity. It is meant to help understand where to start. It is meant to let you know that, while you may feel alone, many of us have walked that same path. Despite it being less than a direct path, it is worth both your time and your talent.

A Guide for New Leaders

The field of leadership is one of the most written-about and published domains in the book world, but there are few relatable guides for novice leaders about what the challenge is like, what they will encounter, what they should do, where to start, and what exciting things will materialize after weeks and months of struggle.

One can read plenty about what Jack Welch or Sheryl Sandberg or Richard Branson did to turn their businesses into globally recognized and powerful brands. But new leaders need more than just stories. They need a guide and a plan. *Making Remarkable* is meant to provide a guide to the things that any new leader should be thinking about as they assume the role for the first time.

I also wrote the book because the leadership journey, particularly for those embarking on it for the first time, is lonely—even when you have the support of friends, family, peers, and your board. You can ask millions of questions of peers, mentors or others, but the reality is that when you are sitting at your desk, or your computer, or in front of that employee you are about to fire, it is all on you. And doing that for the first time can be lonely and scary and confusing.

Leaders aren't born, they are built over time—through experience, challenge, learning, drive, persistence and humility. Not everyone can be a leader. Not everyone *should* be a leader. Being a leader is not simply having the title. As Cal Newport suggests in *So Good They Can't Ignore You*, you cannot get to a position of leadership and responsibility just by putting in the time or performing the role. You need to get so good that you're too good to ignore. That takes focus and commitment. And the journey never ends.

A Guide to Achieving Remarkability

The second reason I wrote *Making Remarkable* was because I believe passionately that so many organizations around the world do <u>good</u> work but have the potential to do <u>remarkable</u> work and truly tackle amazing challenges and improve lives, if only they could make the organizational improvements necessary.

My purpose, and a huge reason for writing *Making Remarkable*, is to inspire leaders to transform their organizations so that they can become remarkable and improve the world.

Making Remarkable came to be because there was a gap. I knew we had to change things at the Calgary Chamber. I needed to overhaul the whole thing. But I couldn't just shut it down and remodel. We had to keep the organization open and running—kind of like refinishing a plane while it's flying. To do that, I needed a guide, a plan. A plan that not only outlined what we needed to do but the state we needed to achieve. I looked. That guide just didn't exist. So, I put it together. *Making Remarkable* is that guide, addressing the key elements of any organizational transformation or improvement.

Why change and transformation? Because the reality is that if you lead an organization like a chamber, association or (frankly) any small or mid-sized entity—for or non-profit—you likely need a transformation to achieve remarkability. The world is changing, and the competition intensifying, so quickly that your organization probably did not keep up with the times. Hence your mandate or desire, I can comfortably assume, includes transformation into a "modern" organization, the "organization of the 21st Century"—or, as I like to call it, the *remarkable* organization.

Is *Making Remarkable* applicable to you only if you're totally changing everything in the organization? No, it is as relevant if you're changing even one part of your organization as it is if you were tasked with gutting the place and starting over from scratch. *Making Remarkable* is a guide to the major parts of a remarkable organization and what a leader should look at, think about and do to change each of those parts. If you need to change only one part—great! *Making Remarkable* can help. If you need to change absolutely everything *Making Remarkable* is for you, too.

This book is not the result of research on thousands of organizations, or hundreds of hours of interviews with CEOs. It's based on successful lived experience. What frustrates me about so many of the top business books is that they are written by professors or consultants who have never implemented a thing in their life. *Making Remarkable* bucks that trend; the practices here have been forged in the fires of experience and refined and improved over time. They are battle tested.

Making Remarkable is written from one person's perspective, grounded in the world of non-profit organizations, specifically chambers of commerce, associations, or member-based organizations. Your leadership or transformation journey may look somewhat different and may take place in any kind of organization or business, for-profit and non-profit alike. The legal form, focus or approach is immaterial. This book is for people who want to break from the pack and are determined to make their organization remarkable.

So, if you're a new leader, someone taking on the top job for the first time, and/or are tasked with transforming your organization into something remarkable and fit for complexity, I hope that I can help support your journey.

Who Am I to Write *Making Remarkable*?

Fast forward six months from my meeting with the headhunter and the job was mine. I had convinced the selection committee and board that they should gamble on me to transform this 121-year-old organization. To their credit, the board of the Calgary Chamber at the time had wanted transformation. That was a huge advantage for me that many leaders won't have— they must work to convince the board of the need for change. In fact, the Calgary Chamber board had recently completed a study that outlined what they needed to transform and hiring an under-40 (I was 35 when I was hired) was a key first step in demonstrating the shift toward becoming a more modern organization.

When I started as CEO, the Calgary Chamber was struggling. It had a brand problem. Its team wasn't operating at top performance. It was losing money on many business lines. It had a board of 20 people and around 1,500 members. It used outdated systems (some of its IT platform was *literally* stuck together with duct tape). It had no rigor or process in terms of its hiring, contracts, or document management. It had a bland and generic mission statement and lacked a solid value proposition.

In short, it was not yet remarkable. But that was recognized, and my job was to get it there.

When I left the organization as President and CEO at the end of 2017, I left the Chamber far better than I found it. While we were never "done" or "there"—I don't believe that you ever are—the Calgary Chamber is now vastly improved. Through the hard work of me and my colleagues, supported by our board, we:

- Turned a struggling organization into a profitable enterprise with a healthy strategic reserve account and a drive to become globally leading in its field

- Rebuilt the brand and created a solid value proposition

- Rebuilt the culture and team into one of skilled people, passionate engagement, a solid values-based HR approach, and where 100% of staff enjoy coming to work (according to the annual staff survey)

- Rebuilt every aspect of the organization, from contracts to IT, systems, finances, policies, bylaws and procedures

- Fostered a performance culture that establishes clear objectives and key results, and regularly assesses performance to help staff improve their skills and achieve their targets

- Achieved recognition, including awards from the World Chamber Federation and the Canadian Chamber of Commerce, and my appointment as Vice Chair of the Association of Chamber of Commerce Executives Board, the first non-American to hold that post in its 100-year history

Despite all this success, within these pages I have tried to be honest and direct. I have tried to share my failures, mistakes and errors with you just as much as sharing some successes. I have tried to be honest about what worked and what did not. I'm not perfect, and neither were my decisions and actions. Chances are, neither will yours be.

I'm a generalist and so, while I recommend that you do many things in this book, I did not do them all myself, nor am I an expert in every part of remarkability. What I am good at is seeing through complexity to create plans and teams that will deliver. For some of the changes we made at the Calgary Chamber, we did hire advisors and consultants, and for those instances I have made note of that. But most of the work I oversaw internally.

Many people say that my teammates and I turned the Calgary Chamber into a remarkable organization. I would like to think we did too. I am grateful to all who supported and joined me along the journey. I hope that the pages ahead will help you make yours remarkable as well.

How *Making Remarkable* is Organized

Making Remarkable is organized into two parts:

1. The first part is about leadership, understanding the nature of change, assessing your organization, creating a plan to transform, and the process to get approval for making your organization remarkable.

2. The second part gets into the detail of the three pillars of remarkability—Purpose, People and Platform, each

broken down into their elements—including a snapshot for why each pillar and element is important, where to start your transformation, and a resource kit that includes diagnostic questions, so you can assess the actual state of your organization compared to the desired state, and other helpful tools and sources for further learning.

The book closes with a framework to ensure that, once your organization becomes remarkable, it stays remarkable.

PART 1: Leadership and Remarkability

CHAPTER 2: Leading the Remarkable Organization

Congratulations! You've done it. You've convinced a group of people that you are the right person for the top job. You've spent a lot time preparing for this day—the day you walk in as a President and CEO, or an Executive Director, for the first time.

What is it like? It's pretty damn exciting.

And scary. And intimidating. And rewarding. And confusing. And exhausting. And inspiring.

Having achieved the top role in my career, I can say that, it is an incredible privilege and responsibility that I have never regretted taking on.

This chapter aims to provide insight and perspective into what it will be like to sit in the top chair. It shares the traits and characteristics that you'll need to cultivate if you're going to thrive in a leadership role. It will cover what you will face in the role, and it will give you a sense of where to turn when you need help.

Regardless of where you are in your journey, how long it took you to get there, or how long you have been in the role, I hope that this book helps shed some light on the nature of the role.

Your Leadership Style

Some people confuse the notion of leadership with a title, or a status, or a role in and of itself. But leadership is a practice and a continual journey, not a position or station.

Many people seek the top role simply because they seek leadership as a position—they want power and authority. To my way of thinking, that's the wrong perspective and the wrong motivation. Leadership is all around us. It is what people do, not what's on their business card. It is forged on the anvil of time and experience, not granted by virtue of a title or authority. It is gained through effort and energy, discipline and dedication. In fact, I believe you can't teach leadership. The only real teacher of leadership is experience and practice.

I have often been asked about my leadership style.

It's important to know that there is no "right" style or approach to being a leader. Many books and resources will tell you differently—that they have interviewed the CEOs of top performing organizations over the past three decades and they can identify six traits of ideal leaders, or three habits, or twenty behaviours. But the truth is that every situation, context and dynamic requires a different type of leader and leadership style. World War II required different leadership than the Iraq War. An organization on the brink of closure requires different leadership than one that is on the cusp of going exponential. There are as many different leadership styles as there are organizations, and only you can determine what kind of leader you want to be, and in what situations and ways you want to lead.

Do you want to lead in times of growth or turnaround? Do you want to lead in times of crisis or calm? Do you want to lead in the spotlight or in the shadows? Do you want to be directing or collaborative? Do you want to celebrate or get down to work?

There are no right or wrong answers to these questions, but they all have implications for the kinds of organizations you will lead, the situations under which you will lead, and the kinds of people and outcomes that you will attract. The only leadership guidance I will provide here is that you need to develop a sense of your preference for your leadership focus and about how and when you want to lead.

After a couple of decades of leadership roles, I have concluded that I am a leader that likes to fix or change things but doesn't enjoy it as much when things are just cruising. My approach is collaborative and engaging but direct, demanding and discerning, and I take an immense amount of ownership of all that I do. If you had asked me early on, before I had more leadership experience, to describe my preferred style and situation, I would not have been able to do so. That kind of perspective took time and experience.

I'm still growing, learning and developing as a leader. I was bad at it in the beginning, despite having some excellent mentors and role models. I always thought that it was going to be easier than it actually is. I began as too passive and didn't hold people to account. Then I began to try and crack down. Then I swung a bit more back to a middle ground.

The other thing to remember about a leadership style is that you don't have to try and be everything that everyone needs every minute of the day. Trying to play every single leadership role whenever someone wants or needs it comes across as disingenuous and unnatural.

For example, I am not much of a celebrator of things—it doesn't come naturally to me. Like Harvey Specter from *Suits* claims: "I don't have dreams, I have goals. Now, it's on to the next one." I am driven by accomplishment and when I am done, I move on. I work at the whole celebrating thing, but I also build complementary supports on my team that make up for this shortcoming. I have had colleagues who live to celebrate and could rally the team at any time; it was a way for them to dial into their own leadership strengths and back up my shortcomings.

Jack Welch is different from Mary Barra who is different from Mark Zuckerberg who is different from Indra Nooyi. Your current boss, or past boss, was different from the person before them, and is different from the next person who will come along. Don't try to force a style that isn't yours. Many people are held up as exemplary leaders. But you are not them. I can assure you they had their faults and shortcomings, too. Develop your own style. Think about how and when you want to lead and find people to model. Test and iterate—this is a theme that will run through *Making Remarkable*—to see what works, how you feel, how people respond, and what outcomes you generate.

What Will it Be Like to Sit in the Chair?

Almost everyone is an armchair leader, because leading looks easy, rewarding, and awesome. The reality is different.

Like everything, leadership has its moments, and, like intoxication, it is hard to describe till you get there yourself. You will likely have experienced aspects of the top role in your rise to it, say as a VP or director in charge of a department, etc. But, having the top job is different even from that.

It's Emotional

The role of leadership can be incredibly emotional. From the highs of accomplishment to the pits of failure, it is that and everything in between. You'll probably develop a sense of ownership over everything about the place: what gets done, how it gets done, when it gets done, and you will bring with that sense of ownership a variety of expectations and emotions.

You will have moments of intense pride as your team steps up and hits a homerun. Whether that is in the form of an event, a sale, a paper, a program, advocacy, new business, satisfied customers or members, or operations in general, you will find yourself in a moment of success that creates intense pride. You will love those moments, so cherish them, and let the team know when they have done well.

I can recall some intensely emotional moments. From the highs of a perfect presentation, an amazing endorsement from a member or landing a large sponsorship, to the lows of an employee betrayal, a missed target or the disappointment of an important customer. Unless you're a robot, these moments and situations will be emotional.

I came into the role with far too high a set of expectations about how easy it would be to transform the Calgary Chamber, and a totally unrealistic sense of how quickly it would happen. I encountered many obstacles, such as a disengaged staff, colleagues with complicated agendas, and a limited budget. I wasn't prepared for as much of this as I encountered, and for the first year or so I was in a very negative emotional state.

It's a Pressure Cooker

People will have high expectations of you. They will be waiting for you to make decisions and bring about change. They will be watching to see how you respond and the ways in which you make your decisions. They will be looking for answers and have been waiting for you to arrive, so they can get on with some of their own work.

The role looks easy from further down the corporate hierarchy. "I will do it differently when I'm the CEO," people often say. I myself have done it many times. "When I am a leader, I will do this and this, but never that." Take it from me: it is much, much easier to be an armchair leader than it is to live that leadership role, to deliver and make the tough choices. You'll experience an intense of amount of pressure to make the right decisions, do the right thing, model the path, create results.

When you're the leader, there's no one higher than you that people can go to. You can't pawn a decision off to someone else. When the board wants answers to their tough questions on poor performance, you can't call in sick that day, or say that's not your department. It *all* rests with you. And that's a lot of pressure. If someone on your team slips up with a key relationship or makes a public relations mistake, it's on you to take that bullet.

In my early days, there were many tough finance and audit committee meetings, in which I was grilled by the board on poor financial performance. Meetings like that are just plain tough. You feel the pressure and there's nowhere to hide. Once, I asked a department lead to join a meeting to answer the committee's questions; after getting grilled much like I had been getting for months, he proclaimed that the chair was a jerk and that he didn't want to go to those meetings anymore. In the top role, you don't have that off-ramp. I've taken responsibility for everything from everyday staff errors to speakers who cut off sponsors who had paid five figures to introduce them. Not easy and not pleasant, but that's part of the job.

People Will Surprise You

While the arrival of a new leader is often heralded as a good thing, not everyone will support you. They may have lost out on the job themselves, they may worry about their security, they may have been tight with the previous leader, or they may just not like the look of you or the sound of your voice. Whatever it is, some people will just have it in for you. There is nothing you can do about that. You must decide whether you want to try and turn them around, or whether they just aren't a fit for the team. Just don't expect everyone to be throwing you a party from the start.

And people will surprise you. Former naysayers will become champions. You will get appreciation from a place you never thought you would. The people who sing your praises may not be who you expect them to be.

Some staff will surprise you on certain days by delivering more than you thought they could, and other days the people who you count on to deliver just mail it in. There is, at times, no rhyme or reason as to how people will show up other than to acknowledge that they are human. And we all have our days.

I can recall many situations where people surprised me. The note of appreciation from someone whom I didn't feel I had made much of an impact on. The dressing down from someone I thought was firmly on my side. Or the disloyalty from someone I'd spent years supporting and cultivating. As the top leader, you will likely experience such things, so don't be surprised when they happen.

It Requires Patience and Empathy

Maybe you're like me; not very patient. I can't stand waiting. I like to take quick action and get things done. But in your leadership role, you'll need to have patience. People and projects won't move as quickly as you would like. People don't have the same sense of ownership or urgency that you have and leaning on them often doesn't build morale and even causes people to burn out.

You will get a lot of stuff dumped on your desk. People issues. Toxic behaviours. I don't like this person. I want a better office. I have this little problem. I don't get it. I have an idea for an event. I'd like to introduce myself because I think my presentation on sales would be perfect for your membership. I want to sell you something. Can I buy you a coffee and pick your brain?

All of this and more will hit your desk or inbox. You will get dragged into more stuff than you ever thought possible, and even more so the smaller the organization and team. You will run out of time for your work because you are meeting with everyone else.

Be patient, with yourself and with your team. But do set boundaries around what is acceptable and what is not, and what/who you will give time to and what you will not. Other people's priorities are not your priorities, so you will need to set those boundaries. Some will try and pass the monkey on their back onto yours. Demonstrate patience and empathy. But don't take their monkey.

It's Lonely

I have found that being CEO is a lonely role. It's not that you are completely bereft of human interaction, but you often don't have your finger on the pulse like you used to. People are a bit reluctant to let their guard down with you. They'll tell you what they think you want to hear, not what they want to tell you. There is no peer in your organization that you can go and commiserate with. You are expected to be able to handle it all.

I can recall at times when something has been going on and I have been totally oblivious to it—divorces, upset about a new policy, struggles between colleagues, team lunches. Maybe this says something about me. But I also know that people don't always want the boss around because it changes the dynamic. I have also found that when I ask direct questions, of junior staff in particular, I haven't always felt that I was getting the straight goods. And that's okay, I get it: talking to the CEO can be intimidating, no matter how many times you try to make people feel comfortable. I've learned to respect all of this; people need space to connect, engage and vent and they don't always feel free to speak their minds to the top person. Try not to take it personally. But do build and access your safety net (to be discussed shortly).

It's About Thinking Big

If you have been a department head prior to the top job, you've had the luxury (at least some of the time) of thinking just of your department and your team. Being in the top role will require you to think and act more broadly, deeply and laterally. You must fight for and defend the entire organization.

You must learn to be more collaborative and to work in ways that reach across and into different parts of the organization and groups of stakeholders. At all times you will need to balance the competing demands of your leadership team, who are responsible for their own domains. You'll be called on to act as referee, conductor, coach and mentor. You will have to make some tough calls about priorities, preferences, allocation of resources, and to manage the fact that in such circumstances someone will win, and someone will lose. All you can do is make the best decision you can with the information you have, and then provide your rationale for that decision. Not everyone will like it, but if you do it well, they will respect it.

Once you are in the top job, you will need to do what is in the best interest of the organization for the long term. You must think big picture, wide angle and long term.

Remarkable Leadership Requirements

The section above provided a small snapshot of some of the things that books on leadership skills won't tell you; only experience can teach you such lessons.

Below are a few traits that leaders aiming for remarkability will need to develop. They are the characteristics that you will need if you're going to thrive in the practice of leadership, and particularly on a difficult project such as transformation or increasing the remarkability of any organization.

Mindset

You must believe that transformation is necessary and possible. You must have the mindset that change will be hard yet worth the time and effort. Your mindset must be one of willingness to invest in things that may not succeed and giving your team the support they need to try new things. A leader's mindset must now be about creating purpose, culture, values and undertaking experiments that may (or may not) put you into exciting and new territory. It is one of supporting people and letting them deliver on possibility.

Nothing can happen without this mindset. You must know it, believe it, feel it and act on it.

Courage

Courage will be needed to make tough calls on people, events, products, partnerships.

Courage doesn't mean the absence of fear. I have been scared many times about the decisions I was about to make and have lost many nights of sleep over them. Courage is action in the face of that fear.

You will need to find the courage to make those tough calls, despite the pit in your stomach, the worry about affecting someone's livelihood, the people who will no longer talk to you, or the investment at risk. It is scary and gut-wrenching, but without the courage to make the tough calls, your leadership journey risks being a very short-lived one. You will have been hired to drive change, not make friends.

Courage is about resilience: resilience to face struggle, challenge, opposition and failure, and to do it again. And again.

Discipline

Follow the vision and stay the course that you have charted requires a lot of discipline.

This means avoiding shiny pennies, urgent-seeming but actually unimportant issues, and people who will take you off your game. The best way to maintain discipline is to make clear to people or stakeholders the path that you are on, and to develop milestones to reach. Goals and targets in the public domain create an accountability that ensure you maintain discipline.

Live the words of former U.S. Navy SEAL Task Unit Commander Jocko Willink: "discipline equals freedom." Having discipline and sticking to your commitments gives you the freedom to decide what to do and to avoid the strain of wondering what you should be doing.

You will need discipline to hold people accountable for their actions and performance. You will need to be disciplined about continuous improvement. You need to keep growing and improving in your role. Just because you have achieved the top job doesn't mean that you can't improve and keep getting better. Michael Jordan, Serena Williams, and Tessa Virtue never stopped practicing and improving. Neither should you.

Acceptance

Accept the challenges, the opposition (even the dislike) that will come. You'll make many decisions in your leadership role and/or in transformation. Some will be popular, and others won't be. Some people will be mad at you about the decisions you make. You will need to develop the ability to be okay with that. Making decisions and then personalizing or internalizing the consequences will give you insomnia. Ultimately, you must be at peace with yourself over your decisions.

Health

The new leadership role, particularly under a change-and-transformation mandate, can take a significant toll on the body and mind. Recognize that change will take time and will be exhausting and challenging. Going into it with the right frame of mind is crucial to your eventual success.

I went into my first top leadership role with rose-coloured glasses, an unrealistic timeline and a sense of optimism. I wasn't prepared for the challenges and the opposition, and they hit me hard, mentally and emotionally. I went into a pretty dark place. In retrospect, I see that my mental health would have been better had I had more realistic expectations.

And don't forgo your physical well-being. New leadership and change can be a recipe for early mornings, long days, lots of meals out and a ton of stress. And that is the perfect recipe for weight gain and illness. Take care of your body: eat properly, get some exercise, and jealously guard the time you need to disconnect from work.

Will

You must be willing to cut things—including programs, budgets, old ways of doing things, sometimes even people. Have no sacred cows. An unwillingness to cut things means you will never achieve your highest leadership potential, or the organization's potential. You will be stuck in old ways, hitching a ride to irrelevance.

Be willing to abandon tradition. Just because it has always been done one way is no reason to justify the continued existence of bad/poor/unprofitable/stale things.

Be willing to take a stand for the things that you believe in. The world needs more strong, values-based, ethical leaders. Be one of those.

Be persistent. Persistence is the manifestation of the will to continue in the face of continued challenge, struggle, disappointment and even failure. Sometimes persistence is the difference between success and failure.

Adaptiveness

You will need to be adaptive to uncertainty, complexity and multiple options. The amount of change in the world is intense, and the range of options you will be faced with is vast. Challenges will not be simple; they will be interconnected and deep. You will need to be comfortable operating in that space.

Generosity

I found that the organization performed better when we gave to others – when we gave away ideas, templates, material, plans etc. I'm not talking about giving stuff away for free like tickets or memberships. I am talking about when a chamber from another city called and asked for our strategic plan, or our bylaws, or our membership model. Sharing and giving is a key part of making your organization and those around you stronger and better. Give freely and give often without asking for anything in return. It makes everyone better.

Your Safety Net: Where to Turn

Leadership can be a lonely and uncertain role. You won't have all the answers, and this book doesn't have all the answers, either. You're going to need someone to turn to for help, guidance and counsel.

This support network will be your safety net to help in growth, development, ideas and in times of challenge or uncertainty.

Your Board

In an ideal world, your board would be prepared to support you in your journey and to provide guidance and counsel on matters of leadership. The challenge with engaging your board is that you may worry about their assessment of you and your capabilities. This will depend on the board overall, the individual board members you engage, and the types of issues you bring to them.

I was fortunate in that I had some excellent leaders on my board when I joined, specifically my friend and mentor Simon Vincent, who was the chair when I was hired. He spent countless hours coaching me on the issues that the Calgary Chamber was facing, provided some strategic options for solving them, and gave me great advice on leadership principles and approaches. All my subsequent chairs—to whom I am grateful—were incredibly supportive and gave so much time and great advice over the years.

You may not feel comfortable exposing your lack of experience or confidence in certain decision domains to your board. That's just fine—there are other places you can turn.

Mentors and a Personal Board

I have been fortunate to find many thoughtful and insightful mentors throughout my career, upon whom I can call when I need guidance or am facing a dilemma.

Consider asking people whose insights, perspective and experience you respect and can learn from to serve as informal mentors. The informal part is important because that makes it more casual, in that they don't expect to have to buy you breakfast once a month. Ask them to be there if you have any questions or if issues that arise you would like their feedback on. Promise not to bug them.

A mentor does not have to be more senior than you in age or role. In fact, it is often positive to find someone younger, who might be more dynamic or experienced in, say, social media or technology, than you to serve as a mentor. I have a few mentors who are younger than me, but I always feel that their perspective is so valuable that age or years of experience are irrelevant.

You may find value in creating a personal cabinet or advisory board, separate from any board of directors that you report to, that includes people selected and invited by you who can advise you on the directions and actions you are contemplating in your role. This might be a table of mentors, but it may also be others whose roles in the community you value or respect but who are not formal mentors to you. This is clearly a more structured and formal approach so, depending on what you're looking for, the way you engage these advisors will be different.

Peers

I may have mentioned that it's lonely at the top. And the only people who know what you're experiencing, or have gone through that challenge, are peers—people with the same role, title and responsibility as you.

I have found a network of peers to be an incredible source of support and guidance for me to this very day. It is like group therapy, peer learning and comic relief all wrapped up in one package.

I view the peer situation in two ways: peers within your professional community (i.e., they work for an identical organization to you—so for me it was other CEOs of chambers of commerce) or peers within your geographic community (i.e., CEOs of local organizations that are not the same kind of organization).

I have approached both professional and geographic community peers in two ways: one-on-one, and in organized peer networks. Both are valuable. I will often call up a peer in the local community and ask if they have encountered a certain challenge. I also met twice a year with my fellow chamber of commerce CEOs across North America to discuss the challenges that we faced. I can't recommend the engagement of peers highly enough. It is one of the best ways to learn, find support and feel connected.

Associations

I am a big believer in the role of an association, whether it is industrial or professional. They have an important role to play in advancing the industry or profession.

As a result, I have been active with the World Chamber Federation, Association of Chamber of Commerce Executives, Chamber of Commerce Executives of Canada, and the Canadian Chamber of Commerce. I have learned a great deal from discussing and collaborating with my peers and colleagues in these associations, which themselves are excellent sources of learning and professional development. The interaction with peers there and informally is also where I have turned often for guidance and support. I encourage you to consider getting involved with your professional or industrial community.

The New Leadership

The practice of leadership is different now than it has been in the past. Leaders of today need to be far more conscious of what they do and how they do it for two main reasons: first is the velocity and complexity of change happening in the world, and the second is the visibility and transparency of leadership. (The velocity and complexity of change will be touched on later in this book, when I discuss some of the massive changes happening in our technological, social, demographic, economic and environmental spheres.)

Leadership is shifting, and leaders must now operate under constant complexity, disruption and adaptation like no other time in history.

Radical changes—such as AI, robotics, and autonomous vehicles—are multidimensional and complex, requiring complete rethinks about what they mean and how to respond to them. And they are changing so fast that a response will evolve the longer one waits to address it. In subsequent chapters, I'll discuss means by which leaders can increase their understanding of, and subsequent organizational response to, the changes in the world, and operate using a continuous practice of surveying, adapting and measuring.

What is critical, however, is that leaders today feel less demand to be the expert or knowledge base for all things for their organization and feel more demand to be the chief convener of expertise and perspectives. No CEO can be an expert anymore on the range of forces affecting their operation—but they can bring a range of people together to help inform and shape the directions of an organization. Strong networks and the ability to convene are essential features of the new leader.

The second reason leadership has changed is that it is now open and social. You must assume that, at any moment, what you do or say can be caught on a phone and distributed via multiple social media channels instantaneously. Your past and private life can be dug into and posted for the world to see and comment on. Pictures and words shared years ago are fair game for public disclosure. While to err is human, you will need to be particularly diligent to ensure that nothing you do, say or publish can be interpreted to put yourself or your organization in bad light.

But with the realities of transparency and access, we are also seeing the positive. We are seeing unethical leaders fall. People in positions of authority or dominance, like Harvey Weinstein, who have felt they could commit unacceptable and unethical acts with no repercussions, are now paying the price as people come forward and share their experiences. Movements like #MeToo and #BlackLivesMatter are reshaping humanity and leadership for the better. But it should not take the victims coming forward to bring an end to that kind of thought and behaviour. Leaders today must themselves perform at the highest ethical standard and make it clear that they will not tolerate inappropriate and unethical behaviour in their organization. And then they must model that every day.

I experienced something akin to this in my time as a CEO. I was faced with a staff member of authority who had been conducting themselves inappropriately with other staff. That person was dismissed immediately, and the whole organization underwent a process of healing and structural and attitude changes at the office to ensure that people knew what was and what was not acceptable. As a leader, you will need to set the expectations of behaviour and model them for your team.

You Set the Tone and Model the Way

As CEO or leader of the organization, it is up to you create remarkability. You won't do it all, but you must set the tone and model the way. You need to be the driver. The evangelist. You need to set the standards. You must get people inspired. Talk about what it will be like; talk about why it will be better. Show people the way.

You will need to have the drive, determination and diligence necessary to become remarkable, and to stay there. Your tone and your actions, your words and your commitments, will create the space for people to try and experiment; to push forward in achieving remarkability as a team. To test and to iterate. To know what is acceptable and what is not. If your board, team and members don't feel that you truly believe it, or that you aren't committed to it, then they won't be on side. You will need to be the one who pulls them up during times of struggle or failure. You will need to be their inspiration and their light.

Leaders must be there to support their team—in understanding, in change, in development, and in transformation. Through creating an environment that is rooted in purpose, supported by values and embracing possibility, leaders will create the space for their organizations to work, and test, and try, and build. All in an effort to achieve remarkability.

You can try as hard as you like but if you don't set the tone and model the way, no other part of the puzzle will fall into place. You won't get the right people. You won't make the right choices or the right investments. You just won't get there.

At a time when we are seeing too many failures of leadership, you need to model what is and is not acceptable in your organization—in terms of values, behaviour, jokes, interactions, relationships, performance, deadlines, creativity, innovation, inspiration, engagement, and more. If you want, and need, a team that will push boundaries, work hard, dig deep, act ethically, deliver on a purpose and values, hold each other accountable, and overall achieve remarkability, then you, as leader, will need to set that tone and that standard. For you model the way for everyone else.

In the end, getting to remarkable starts with you.

Getting Started

Where you start will depend on where you and your organization are at. If you are a new leader then you have likely heard of the "first 100 days." While the first 100 days are important, and they shouldn't be wasted, you must either be a superhero or have unlimited resources to effect any significant change within 100 days. Don't be excessively hasty.

Don't feel pressured to make massive changes too early. It took me over 365 days to really get to the crux of the matter for some aspects of the business, because it takes a full calendar year to experience such things as an AGM, annual events, budgeting etc. It will take 365 days to see what happens in each of the parts of an annual cycle. Therefore the 100 days thing should be taken with a grain of salt. You risk making rash decisions if you try to do too much too soon.

Determine if there are any situations that need to be addressed immediately. Is there anything that is threatening your organization either overtly or covertly? Those things should make their way to the top of your "to do" list.

So, where to begin? Chapter 3 will go over the characteristics of a remarkable organization and the change happening in the world—so you can understand what you are aiming for and the scale and span of change occurring.

Chapter 4: The Remarkability Agenda clearly lays out the steps to follow to assess your organization and its current state. It then details how to build your plan for change—the Remarkability Agenda—and then provides a proven process to get it approved.

Chapters 5-12 go through all eight elements of remarkability in detail, so you know what you are aiming for.

At the end of the book, Chapter 13, is a model that you can use after you have completed your Remarkability Agenda in order to stay remarkable. Remember: being remarkable is not an end state but a regular practice.

Resource Kit

Ask This

- What leadership style do I want to develop?
- Do I know how, and in what kinds of situations, I want to lead?
- Who do I want to emulate?
- Who can I call upon for mentorship, guidance and support?
- How can I best prepare myself for the realities of leadership?
- What will I define as my ethical leadership approach, and what will I make clear is unacceptable on our team?

Do This to be Remarkable

- Seek out mentors to help you learn and grow.
- Read, watch and listen a lot.
- Talk to other people to learn from peers.
- Manage expectations – yours and others
- Be realistic – don't wear rose coloured glasses but don't be a total cynic.
- Seek out a variety of supports to help learn, grow and share.
- Don't doubt yourself.

Review This

- James M. Kouzes and Barry Z. Posner, *The Leadership Challenge*. Jossey-Bass (2007).
- James Macgregor Burns, *Transforming Leadership*. Atlantic Monthly Press (2003).
- Thomas J. Neff and James M. Citrin, *You're In Charge – Now What? The 8 Point Plan*. Three Rivers Press (2005).

- Jack Welch, *Winning*. HarperCollins (2005).
- Phil Knight, *Shoe Dog: A Memoir By the Creator of Nike*. Scribner (2016).
- Howard Schultz, *Onward: How Starbucks Fought for Its Life without Losing Its Soul*. Rodale (2011).
- Cal Newport, *So Good They Can't Ignore You: Why Skills Trump Passion in the Quest for Work You Love*. Grand Central (2012).

CHAPTER 3: The Remarkable Organization

The harsh reality is that very few organizations are remarkable. Many have let too much change pass them by and have not adapted. Many don't have a clear purpose. Some have had bad leadership that made bets in the wrong places. Some have hired the wrong people who don't have a drive for remarkability. Others have a poorly defined value proposition or business model and can't make a go of it. Some have failed to understand the needs of their customer and have built programs or services that no one wants. And some still hold onto outdated history and legacy that weigh them down like anchors. Any of these will make an organization average or mediocre.

Fortunately, that doesn't need to be you. Within these pages you will find the guide, the plan, the framework and the approach to beat the odds and be a remarkable organization.

So why would you want to put in the work to be remarkable? Because it's worth it. Remarkability is what separates the uncommon and extraordinary from the merely good, suitably adequate and the intensely mediocre. Remarkability is what gets results, noticed, support, interest, funded and wins. Therefore, leaders committed to getting their organizations to do their absolute best and finest work strive to make their organizations remarkable.

Why is becoming remarkable so difficult? It is because it takes constant adaptation and evolution to the changing world and the resulting needs and challenges faced by your customer or member. We are surrounded by multiple and complex changes, like rising populism. We are surrounded by socio-demographic changes, like baby boomers beginning to retire and millennials taking a more substantial role in the workforce. Or increasing income inequality. Or technological changes that are introducing tools, experiences and opportunities that even two years ago we never thought possible. Or environmental changes that are forcing us to think about what we consume and what we use in our daily lives. The list goes on.

In short, we are amid that oft-used word: disruption. Everything is being disrupted. Books. Music. Taxis. Hotels. Banks. Manufacturing. You name it, it's ripe for disruption—including your organization. You must consider that someone somewhere is actively trying to figure out a way to disrupt all or a part of your entire organization.

This change creates the complexity and difficulty in achieving remarkability not only in keeping up with the change, but in determining how it affects your customer and therefore how you and your value proposition should adapt to best meet their needs. It is a complex and ongoing task. That is why remarkability is so difficult. While constant change is a challenge to keep up with, it also creates opportunity to take advantage of and expand your value proposition to meet new and unmet needs. So, while it can disrupt, the change can create new opportunity, value and impact.

Becoming and staying remarkable requires that leaders constantly monitor the changes happening in and around them, and ensure that their organizational purpose, people and platform evolve and adapt to best meet the needs of their customer and member needs today and tomorrow.

Faced with this scope of change, leaders now face a decision: do I get by, or do I aim for remarkable? If you want to get by, you should probably just stop reading here. But, if you want to achieve remarkability, keep reading.

Before we get into fully defining remarkability, let's go through a high-level scan of the kind of change that every organization is currently facing.

The Nature of Change

There are a large variety of resources available to help orient you in understanding the breadth and range of change taking place in the world today. Some will speak to struggle, while others will speak of abundance.

Many of the changes happening are easier to comprehend, like demographic change, while others have vast and far-reaching— and as yet, not fully understood—implications for the future, like blockchain technologies. You can't understand them all, or their implications, but you will need to understand the range of them to help make strategic decisions as to what your organization will face, and how it can respond.

To me, as I write this in the first half of 2018, the two largest issues facing our future are our people and our planet. If we further erode the capability and quality of either, we will continue to face an uneven world in terms of wealth, prosperity, climate, diversity and inclusion, aging populations, global migration and work. Our climate is fragile with incidents of extreme weather events rising every year, yet the ability to address energy and resource needs affordably and in sufficient scale eludes us. Technology is making life easier and harder at the same time; issues of privacy and addiction taking centre stage, but tech is creating new solutions to food, energy, wellness and mobility at the same time. Each day brings new agreements and conflicts around the globe, making it hard to know what regions will create prosperity and what ones will continue to degrade humanity. Understanding all these issues, and knowing what to do about them, is no easy task. It is extremely complex.

One of the best resources out there for making organizations more strategic and modern is *Race for Relevance: 5 Radical Changes for Associations* by Harrison Coerver and Mary Byers, CAE. As I was reading it, I could clearly see myself and the Calgary Chamber in the book's stories and examples. In fact, the book was such a great resource that I brought in Coerver to facilitate a board retreat on governance. (More on that later.)

Coerver and Byers identify six marketplace realities that affect the success of associations and many non-profits:

1. Time: the lack of it and the competition for it
2. Value expectations: ever increasing
3. Market structure: consolidation and specialization
4. Generational differences: the impact of demographic changes
5. Competition: increasing every day from new entrants
6. Technology: its ability to displace many services traditionally offered only by associations

Most leaders in member-based organizations will readily acknowledge these six forces. As a new leader, you will need to understand how they will affect your organization's opportunities and barriers to becoming remarkable.

The extent of global shifts has forced the association world to take notice. In 2016, the Association of Chamber of Commerce Executives (ACCE), under the leadership of then-CEO Mick Fleming, published *Horizon: Chambers 2025*, an exploration of eight trends and forces that will impact chambers of commerce around the world over the next decade. Those forces are:

1. The nature of belonging and gathering
2. Population shift
3. Scarcity and abundance
4. Communications and technology
5. Global impacts
6. Political and social fragmentation
7. Resource alignment
8. Catalytic leadership

While published by, and for, chambers of commerce, the *Horizons: Chambers 2025* report and associated videos are one of the best starting points for understanding the scope and magnitude of change that will affect organizations over the next decade and beyond. These forces are particularly acute for the association and nonprofit world, as many still operate on outdated models and systems, and are competing for an ever-shrinking pool of resources.

Leaders who are determined to lead a remarkable organization must not just stay on top of these changes—they must understand and adapt to them, evolving the organization constantly. Remarkability is a constant process. Leaders must build a practice of surveying, adapting and measuring to stay remarkable; we'll discuss how to build such a practice in Chapter 13.

Mindset: Seeing the Opportunity within Change

To successfully chart an organization's path in times of such potentially overwhelming change, a leader must be open-minded enough to accept that external forces and trends will create pressure for change and are going to affect the organization in some fashion, imaginative enough to understand how change may affect that organization, and capable enough to develop plans for adapting to change to best serve their customer or member. Let's look at each in turn.

First is open-mindedness. It might be easy to sit back and dismiss changes as unimportant trends, fads or situations that will be reversed or addressed by "the market" or by technology. History, however, is not on the side of the dismissive.

Kodak didn't want to acknowledge that the future was in digital images and so spent many years falling behind, only recently re-emerging from bankruptcy as a new company. Smith Corona would not acknowledge that the future was in computers. Blockbuster didn't get that streaming, not real estate, was the future. Many organizations—including chambers of commerce or other member-based associations—spent too many years thinking that people will always want to join and have failed to grasp the scale and magnitude of the changes (demographic, social, technological) that they are facing. All those organizations are now fighting a battle for relevance. A leader must be open-minded about the change that is occurring, and that change will affect their organization. As much as leaders may want to ignore signs, believe that change won't affect them, or that they don't need to change themselves, the truth is that change is like moving water—it finds its way to you eventually. Leaders might as well accept that and then find ways to adapt and build a resilient and dynamic organization to respond and create opportunity.

Next, a leader must be imaginative enough to consider how these changes may affect the organization and consider how to adapt their organization. It is important to re-iterate that the leader need not be an expert in all the change happening, nor have all the answers as to how to chart a course through it, but he or she must act as chief convener—of information, of people, of ideas, of opposing viewpoints—all to paint a series of landscapes, pictures or futures that the organization may face, and to then prepare the organization for one, or a few, of those futures. This ability to convene will be essential, for no leader can know it all anymore. There's just too much change. The leader needs to be able to convene expertise, diverse perspectives and new voices to help chart a path.

Finally, once a leader has considered how the change will affect the organization, they need to be capable of actually making the change. Building and structuring an organization to be flexible enough to adapt and to take advantage of change in order to be best positioned for success is an essential means of achieving this. Leaders can achieve this through their mindset, the clear and compelling purpose and brand that they establish, by the people they hire, and the platforms—particularly value proposition and strategies—they put in place to drive their business forward.

As discussed earlier, this is not a "once and done" practice or approach. The imperative to adapt to change, and the ability to be remarkable, is an ongoing effort and a practice that needs to be implemented by the leadership.

With openness to change thus cultivated, comes the realization that change represents immense opportunity; in fact, more opportunity is being created than destroyed. In his book *Abundance: The Future is Better Than You Think*, Peter Diamandis speaks of a world of abundance—of opportunity, resources—through the adoption and acceleration of exponential technologies, most significantly artificial intelligence, sensors and networks, robotics, digital manufacturing and infinite computing, medicine, and nanotechnology.

Given a positive mindset about the future and opportunities, and adopting these exponential technologies, Diamandis articulates how we can address such global necessities as adequate water, food, energy, transportation, health care and education. The range of potential in just these areas creates immense opportunity for businesses and organizations to lead rather than despair about what is at risk. Organizations and leaders that are not aware of, or do not understand, these disruptions are at risk of fading into irrelevance. Study these changes and technologies. Understand them. See the opportunity in them. Not the loss.

The one option that leaders don't have is to ignore the change. Your value proposition can't remain static. Your members and customers are demanding an organization that delivers them compelling value in the face of change. In the wise words of U.S. Army General Eric Shinseki: "If you dislike change, you're going to dislike irrelevance even more."[1]

The Remarkable Organization: The Three Pillars of Remarkability

Defining the remarkable organization is relatively straight forward. Achieving remarkability is another matter.

There are three pillars to remarkability: Purpose, People, and Platform. Each one of these has several elements under it, all of which must be calibrated for optimal performance, so an organization can deliver its very best work—and achieve remarkability.

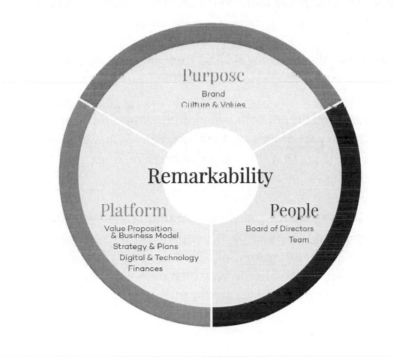

But more than this, a remarkable organization is one that delivers results and impact and is one that peers, competitors and members hold in high regard as uncommon and worthy of notice and commendation. And it is one that creates its own communities and followings. Let's look at each of the pillars in more detail before fully exploring the underlying elements of each pillar in subsequent chapters.

Purpose

Your purpose is your why. Your reason for existence. It is your brand, and your ultimate measure of success. It is astounding how many organizations aren't clear on why they do what they do. They know *what* they do, but they don't know *why* they do it. Remarkable organizations have a clear and compelling purpose that serves as their bedrock, drives them, and attracts followers.

The Purpose pillar's elements and their target state for remarkability are:

- A strong brand, with a clear and compelling purpose, that is part of the organizational DNA, and guides everything that the organization says, does and produces (more in Chapter 5)

- A strong values-based culture that reflects the purpose, spirit and energies of its people, and that guides hiring, development, recognition and rewards programs to attract and retain the very best personnel (more in Chapter 6)

People

People are the driving force behind any remarkable organization. If the right people are on board to govern, work for, and support an organization, that organization will have little to stop it. No matter what strategies are in place, if the right people are not deeply engaged, committed, collaborating, remarkability will remain elusive.

The People pillar's elements and their target state for remarkability are:

- A high-performing board of directors that is focused on the future, strategy and governance, has the right people addressing the right issues, and has the right policies and procedures to ensure that they stay high-performing now and into the future (more in Chapter 7)

- A remarkable team that believes in the organization's purpose, and lives the brand and values each day, operating under a robust leadership operating system and program of development and performance management (more in Chapter 8)

Platform

By platform, I don't mean technology. I mean the way in which an organization activates its purpose and people; the way in which it creates its value, goes to market and operates.

The platforms of a remarkable organization enable the purpose to come to life, and the people to deliver on their task. Remarkable organizations are constantly surveying, adapting and measuring their platforms to make sure that they are current, modern, and meet the needs of their customer. Attempts to become remarkable by focusing only on purpose and people, without adequate attention to the platform, will be like having a well- designed car body and engine, without the transmission, tires or gas.

The Platform pillar's elements and their target state for remarkability are:

- A value proposition that is compelling and perfectly aligned to the needs of a specific target customer or member market, and a business model that supports the profitability of the organization (more in Chapter 9)

- A lightweight and nimble strategy and planning structure that enables creativity, flexibility, accountability and measurement, while creating a line of sight that enables staff to see how their work contributes to the organization's long-term targets (more in Chapter 10)

- A contemporary and well-funded digital and technology approach that enables the enhanced delivery of the value proposition, achievement of organizational metrics and the development and growth of new opportunities, all while making the jobs of staff, and customer experiences, easier and more efficient (more in Chapter 11)

- Strong financial footing and performance that enable investment in new growth opportunities and provide stability and security for the future (more in Chapter 12)

This is what a remarkable organization looks like. Achieving these levels of performance for each of the eight elements of the three pillars will mean that your organization truly can be considered remarkable.

When looking at a remarkable organization, you will also find that they are:

- Nimble
- Responsive to disruption and opportunity
- Innovative, constantly experimenting, testing and refining
- Engaging constantly with members, customers, stakeholders and communities
- Inclusive and diverse
- Purpose driven
- Lean and efficient, leveraging external capabilities
- Accepting of failure

Now that we have defined the remarkable organization, let's look at how to create, and gain approval for, a Remarkability Agenda to make your organization remarkable.

Resource Kit

Ask This

- Do I understand the trends and forces that affect my organization?
- How can I build a practice of surveying the trends and forces affecting my organization?
- Do I have access to people and resources that can help me understand the forces and trends that are affecting my organization?
- Do I have a sense of what state my organization is in? Is my organization tuned to what is needed to achieve remarkability?
- What areas—purpose, people, platform—need the most work?
- Does my organization have the characteristics of a remarkable organization? For example, is it nimble, innovative, purpose-driven, inclusive and efficient?

Do This to be Remarkable

- Be a student.
  - ○ Identify the forces and trends that impact your organization and how to become more knowledgeable about them.
  - ○ Learn and read about diverse forces that are affecting your organization and your customers and members.

- Be a convener.
  - ○ Find people and resources who can help inform your understanding of the trends and forces affecting your organization.

Review This

- BOOKS
  - ○ Jeremy Gutsche, *Better and Faster: The Proven Path to Unstoppable Ideas.* Crown Business (2015).
  - ○ Harrison Coerver and Mary Byers, CAE, *Race for Relevance: 5 Radical Changes for Associations.* ASAE The Centre for Association Leadership (2011).
  - ○ Peter Thiel, *Zero to One: Notes on Startups, or How to Build the Future.* Crown Business (2014).
  - ○ Peter H. Diamandis & Steven Kotler, *Abundance: The Future is Better Than You Think.* Free Press (2012).
  - ○ Peter H. Diamandis & Steven Kotler, *Bold: How to Go Big, Create Wealth, and Impact the World.* Simon & Schuster (2015).
  - ○ Tim O'Reilly, *WTF: What's the Future and Why It's Up to Us.* Harper Collins (2017).

- OTHER
  - ○ ACCE Horizons Chambers 2025 Report www.acce.org/main/horizon-initiative-chambers-2025/
  - ○ McKinsey Global Institute www.mckinsey.com/mgi/overview
  - ○ World Economic Forum www.weforum.org/reports

CHAPTER 4: The Remarkability Agenda

While travelling, I often enjoy wandering around and discovering new and exciting places. I love wandering into little streets, parks or spots organically. This approach may hold for my travel preferences, but the reality is that trying to make an organization remarkable can't be done organically and through random discovery. We all operate on such limited timeframes, budgets and resources that we must ensure we are efficient stewards of time and money. Therefore, you need a plan that clearly lays out where you are and what needs to get done to achieve remarkability. This plan, or guide, to remarkability is called the Remarkability Agenda.

The Remarkability Agenda is the plan for reshaping or reinventing the organization, in whole or in part, to bring about remarkability. To refresh your memory, I earlier spoke of some of the myriad benefits of becoming a remarkable organization as being increased revenue, increased impact and relevance, and increased employee retention and attraction, among many others. Remarkability is rewarding and can generate new value, goodwill and engagement.

The concept of achieving remarkability, and the often-necessary organizational transformation required to achieve it, can be intimidating—vast and uncertain, complex, time consuming and costly. Some of the change along the journey may consist of minor tweaks and adjustments, while some of it may involve major transformations, overhauls and complete rebuilds of structure and offering. You may be thinking about the difficulty of merely gaining approval, or achieving staff buy-in, to do any change, let along making the change itself. Don't let these concerns deter you from achieving true organizational potential and impact. All the best things in life are hard work.

Getting onto the path of change and transformation to remarkable requires four distinct steps which will be covered in this chapter:

1. Assessing your Organization
2. Building your Remarkability Agenda
3. Gaining Approval
4. Implementing the Agenda

Assessing your Organization

Determining how your organization needs to change to become remarkable can be broken into two components: the big picture and the specifics of the three pillars. The three-pillar assessment will dig into each of the eight elements that comprise the pillars and is done using the diagnostic questions at the end of each chapter—so it is meant to give you a comprehensive and detailed evaluation of the specifics.

The big picture assessment will give you a high-level overview of the entire organizational performance currently, historically, against peers, and in the eyes of your most important stakeholders. Assessing both the big picture and the specifics will give you an understanding of your organization's strengths and weaknesses. Let's first look at the steps needed to assess the big picture so that you can start to build your Remarkability Agenda.

The Big Picture

The big picture is a snapshot at a point in time of the performance—past and current—of the organization. It has four elements:

1. Digging into the numbers to assess the financial health of the organization

2. An organizational assessment looking at performance to current plans, KPIs and peer benchmarking

3. Listening to people to get a no-B.S. assessment of what works, and what needs to change

4. An understanding of trends and forces that affect the success of your organization

Dig Into the Numbers

In the interview process, you likely received a copy of the most recent audited financial statements and were given a high-level view of the financial health of the organization. Now it is time to really dig in and get a handle on things.

To give you a sense of what I am talking about here, let me reflect upon my own experience when I first arrived at the Calgary Chamber. When I arrived, I wanted to see the organization's financial data, not just the monthly financials that went to the board. I wanted to see the analytics that would enable us to determine how our assets were performing.

Nothing of the sort existed. So, I asked to see data, starting with the sales function. Surprisingly, while we had membership sales people, no one had ever run a productivity assessment of the sales team to determine something basic: were they bringing in more than they cost us? That analysis had never been done. When I asked for this analysis, the findings were stark: we were spending more on the sales function than we brought in from the revenue of the sales function. Add to that a low member-retention rate and we were bleeding cash. As a result, I terminated the entire sales team and used the website as the tool by which to generate membership sales while we rebuilt the sales model and team. With this approach, we didn't make much—but we did make money as opposed to losing it. This step enabled me to rebuild the membership sales function and team from the ground up and still make money.

Not only were we poor at making money selling memberships, we were also not great at making money from our food and beverage operations. When I joined the Chamber, we owned a building that had a ground-floor coffee shop, a restaurant on the second floor, and meeting rooms with a catering business on floors two and four. All operated by us. When I asked to see how each cost centre of the business was performing, I learned that this data didn't exist, either. When the CFO did this analysis for us, the results were, once again, illuminating.

Years before, the Chamber had decided to renovate the ground floor of the building, swapping out rent-paying tenants (i.e., an income and cash stream) and replacing them with an "internet cafe." That was a great idea but, sadly, poorly timed, for shortly after the space was finished internet cafes became *passé* and Starbucks became the remote office of the world. We were left with a coffee shop that lost money every single day. Staff were happy because they got nice coffee, but it didn't pay the bills.

The numbers also revealed that the restaurant lost money due to it having a buffet structure yet few diners. We switched to an à la carte menu and aimed to reduce our costs. That worked to some degree, but we were competing with many better restaurants and ultimately the Chamber restaurant never made money.

The only part of the business that *did* make money was our meeting room and catering business. Ideally situated downtown, and with a variety of spaces, we were often busy with room rentals and lunch events.

No one had done the analysis on the food and beverage operations, which meant decisions could have been made well before my arrival to tweak the business in the areas that were performing well (the meeting rooms and catering) and shuttering or repositioning the areas that were not performing well (coffee shop and restaurant). By the time I arrived and tried to do anything, it was like rearranging deck chairs on the Titanic; the damage had been done.

Depending upon the size of the organization you may or may not have access to strong financial or accounting expertise. If you have a finance director or a CFO, you can ask them to do this analysis for you. Otherwise, you may want to consider hiring someone who can do many of these analyses—a CPA, a CFA or another financial expert.

You should consider looking at several financial analyses, including:

- Organizational profitability, current and historical, and departmentally/functionally if possible

- Productivity of revenue-generating resources, such as sales and sponsorship, to determine the net income of all sales revenues brought in versus their cost/expense to the organization

- Retention and conversion rates: how many customers/members repeat business, and how long it takes to get a sale

- Historical cash balance and annual cycles

- Balance of investments/restricted funds and historical returns and balances

- Revenue and expense historical growth rates and cyclicality

- Staff expense percentage of total expenses, and growth in salary expense over time

- Net income and margin of revenue areas (like events and conferences)

- Historical average sale value and per customer expenditures annually

This analysis will give you a sense of the organization's financial health, how effective it is with its money, and what kinds of decisions need to be made to either stop the bleeding or continue the acceleration. Knowing the numbers and the finances is key to establishing priorities in a Remarkability Agenda.

Assess Organizational Performance

This step is all about assessing how the organization performs compared to plans and compared to performance measures and benchmarks.

Start by reviewing any existing strategies and plans. Look at what is currently in place and where you are, relative to those plans. You will want to examine any annual plans, budgets, departmental plans and consultant reports that have been prepared for the organization. You'll probably find that some old or outdated strategic plan is in place that may not be relevant to the times or situation. Here you are looking to see what is currently on plan and the current work priorities for the board and your team. This review will help you begin to more clearly see the state of organizational performance and capability.

A key piece of your assessment will be performance against established metrics or targets. Look for any performance indicators or metrics currently being used by the organization and ask for current state and historical data on them. You should be looking at measures such as market penetration; size of organization (budget and FTE) compared to peers; turnover and retention; sectoral representation; and other performance measures.

First, you'll need to assess whether the organization is measuring the right things, and second, whether it is on the correct trajectory for those currently measured indicators. This will help you understand the nature of the performance. Rank the measures in terms of being on track or off track and, with your board and team, dig into why each is the way they are.

To the extent that you can, use peer benchmarking and assess your position against the performance of similar organizations. The Association of Chamber of Commerce Executives (ACCE) offers the Dynamic Chamber Benchmarking tool, an excellent resource to assess the relative performance of a chamber to its peers in terms of revenues, staffing, market penetration and expenses. If this kind of tool exists within your industry, you should take advantage of it. An analysis of yourself by yourself is often limiting in terms of insight, context and comparability. Knowing that you can lift 50 lbs. is great, but you will never know if you should be lifting 100 lbs. until you look at how you compare to others. Benchmarking our chamber to peer chambers helped us understand where we were underperforming and where we needed to improve to be considered best in class.

If this kind of benchmarking service does not exist in your field, you should work to get a sense of how you perform relative to some key indicators that may or may not currently be getting tracked. You can do this by reaching out to some peer leaders in similar organizations and asking if they would share their data in return for your completed analysis. I have done this a few times with everything from salaries and benefits to retention rates and more. I have often found my peers willing to share, and your payback can be offering them the completed analysis, so they can see where they stand relative to other peers.

Listen to People

Once you have generated a picture of organizational performance through data analysis and benchmarking, you should have an informed discussion with a wide range of stakeholders, including:

- Your board
- Your staff and colleagues
- Your customers/members
- Past customers/members
- Your sponsors, patrons or financial backers
- Community leaders
- Naysayers and competition

- Peer organizations (i.e., similar organizations in other cities or locations)
- People whose opinion you trust and respect

Develop a list of the people you want to listen to and get cracking. Make this a priority of your early days. Ensuring that you have diversity of background, perspective and opinion is important as well. Hearing feedback from the echo chamber, or the mutual admiration society, is not particularly useful. You want to have a sufficiently diverse perspective such that it will challenge your assumptions and beliefs.

What you also want here is honesty. I always tell people "don't pat me on the back as I'm walking off the cliff." You want candor—radical candor.

Some questions you should ask include:

- Can you tell me what you think our purpose is, or why you think we exist?
- How are we doing? Are we meeting your needs and expectations?
- What do we do that is really good?
- What do we do that really sucks?
- What do you want to preserve and why?
- What do you want to change/discard and why?
- What do you hope I do?
- What are you concerned I might do?
- What are you concerned I might not do?
- What could I do that would make sure you stayed/joined/returned?
- Who are our biggest competitors and why?
- Who should we collaborate with and why?

- How will you define success for us, and how will you know we got there in years 1, 3 and 5? (This question is oriented to your board and your customers/members.)
- What do you see as a moonshot for the organization?
- Are there any critical or priority issues to address?
- What changes or trends do you see happening that we need to be aware of or should be acting on?

Consolidate your findings and look for themes that emerge; they will help you form ideas and component parts of your Remarkability Agenda. And they can be used to test theories and concepts, as well as to test against data that you have.

Understand Trends and Forces

As a leader you will need to become aware of, and regularly track, those trends and forces that impact your organization's success. As mentioned in the previous chapter, you must cultivate the capacity to accept that change is constantly happening and is likely to affect your organization. You must also have the ability to understand how those changes may affect your organization and be able to choose how to adapt.

This does not mean that you need to become an expert in blockchain, or an authority on AI. But it does mean that you need to make a regular practice of surveying the landscape of the trends and forces that affect the success of your organization, in technology, demographics, health, business, finance, economics, etc. It means engaging with or convening other experts to help build your awareness and understanding. It means trying to have a degree of foresight with respect to what will happen next in certain areas affecting your business, and how you might respond.

It can also help to understand what is going on in your industry and beyond. Make it a habit to dig into the publications and communications of industry associations, journals, blogs, vlogs, videos, thought leaders, research bodies and major consultants, which can all be a source of ideas and insight into interesting projects and approaches that have been used in other industries, professions or domains.

For example, our Chamber looked to higher-end hotels and the role of a concierge to make our on-site event registration and check-in processes more effortless experiences. We learned how hotels engaged with travelers to make sure that their needs were taken care of and that the check-in process was smooth, stress-free and informative. We brought that to our events check-in process by creating expedited lines, special lines for sponsors and top-tier members, digital technologies for check-in and badge printing and roving staff able to answer questions or guide the way. Calgary Chamber events have become the benchmark for events in Calgary, with people regularly commenting to me about their enjoyable and effortless experience.

This activity of understanding trends and forces needs to be a routine practice that takes place at least a few times a year. Instill the importance of this practice within your team so that they too can become adept at finding opportunities for the organization to become remarkable. This activity will be discussed in additional detail in Chapter 13 as part of the SAM (Survey, Adapt, Measure) model that is used to maintain remarkability.

Summarizing the Big Picture
Using all this information, you will be able to develop a picture of the current health and overall performance of the

organization and generate insights as to what items might be on your Remarkability Agenda.

As you summarize the work that you have done:

1. Look for themes, major items and critical opportunities or weaknesses that need to be addressed.

2. Look for major strengths and assets that can be used in a more explicit or dynamic way to drive value, be monetized or be leveraged.

3. Explore the nature of the culture and the state of the people and team.

4. Consider your organization's systems and processes and whether they are up to standard.

5. Reflect on financial resources and performance, and whether any major financial changes or improvements are needed.

6. Consider the organization's resilience to tackle current and future challenges.

7. Identify the major competitive threats to your organization and determine your level of capability in taking them on and surviving them.

8. Look for existing or potential strategic partnerships or alliances. Consolidation, mergers and acquisitions are becoming more and more the norm within organizations like chambers and should be considered when that makes make sense.

Gather these considerations and the summaries of your findings into an impactful and concise report or presentation to be used as part of the case for your Remarkability Agenda.

The Specifics of the Three Pillars

The big picture gives you an overview of the entire operation. Looking at the specifics of the three pillars will help you determine what needs to change before your organization can become remarkable, and what is currently adequate.

To assess the specifics of each of the eight elements of the three pillars for your organization, you should:

1. Read through each chapter to understand what you need to do, and be, to be considered remarkable for each element.

2. Complete the diagnostic assessment questions at the end of each chapter to determine if that remarkability element needs attention. Use a rating of Yes=1, No=0. A score of 80% or better indicates that you are likely remarkable in that element. 80% or better across all questions means you are a remarkable organization. (You can complete all diagnostic questions from each chapter online at www.makingremarkable.com. At the end of each set of diagnostic questions, the tool will provide you with a score and a series of recommendations for you based on your score.[2])

3. Create a summary of your diagnostic assessments and rank those organizational pillars from most in need of improvement to least in need.

Once you have completed the diagnostic assessments for the eight elements, you are ready to combine the findings of your big picture analysis and the element diagnostics.

Building Your Remarkability Agenda

Building your Remarkability Agenda requires a clear picture of what is currently working well and what needs work to achieve remarkability.

The matrix template on the following page provides a sample of how to bring the big picture and diagnostic analyses together in a simple format that will enable you to identify where work is needed (You can download a free workable copy of this matrix at www.makingremarkable.com).

The Remarkability Agenda

		Big Picture Insights (List)	Diagnostic Score (% from diagnostic questions in each chapter)	Needing Improvement/Change? (Y/N)	Specific Aspects Needing Change (List)	Priority Ranking (1-3)
Purpose	Brand					
	Culture and Values					
People	Board					
	Team					
Platform	Value Proposition					
	Strategy and Plans					
	Digital and Technology					
	Finances					

Completing the matrix will provide you with a clear and concise picture of what is working well in the organization, and what needs to be changed in pursuit of remarkability. Based on the findings of the big picture analysis and the diagnostic you will make a determination as to whether any aspect of the eight elements needs work. Those things that are working well do not need to form part of the final Agenda, while those things that need to be addressed—either through their lower diagnostic scores or through the big picture insights—will form the core of your Agenda.

Be specific about the areas that need work and improvement. Once you have assessed what needs work, rank them all in priority order, with 1 being high priority and 3 being low priority. While it is best to start with Purpose and move through to Platform, the situation at your organization will be the final determinant of what your priorities are.

Depending on the health and strength of your leadership team, you may want to decide on your priorities yourself or engage your senior colleagues in a strategic conversation as to what the findings in the matrix are telling you and how you should structure the timing and priorities of your Agenda. This can be done using a structure such as that in *Moments of Impact: How to Design Strategic Conversations that Accelerate Change* by Chris Ertel and Lisa Kay Solomon.

With this matrix complete, you will have a priority ordered list of those elements of your organization that require work in order to achieve remarkability. It is now time to craft your Remarkability Agenda.

The Remarkability Agenda is the plan that will help you achieve the end state of remarkability. It is the guide as to what you need to address and the sequence in which to address them.

To build your Remarkability Agenda, take all the items identified and prioritized as needing work from the assessment matrix completed above and bring them forward to the Remarkability Agenda matrix template on the following page (You can download a free workable copy of this matrix at www.makingremarkable.com). The Agenda matrix includes additional information that will help you plan for, and execute, the work needed and will be helpful in terms of gaining approval or support for the work to be done.

	Specific Aspects Needing Change (List)	Target State	Priority Ranking (1-3)	Address Internally or Externally (i.e. consultant)?	Budget	Anticipated Timing	Key Team	Key Partners or Stakeholders	Risks or Challenges
Purpose Brand									
Culture and Values									
People Board									
Team									
Platform Value Proposition									
Strategy and Plans									
Digital and Technology									
Finances									

The Remarkability Agenda matrix should include information such as target state for each element (as outlined in each chapter), how it will be completed (i.e., internally or using a consultant), anticipated cost and timing, and critical team and partners. Any risks or challenges to successful project completion should also be identified.

This simple matrix, supported by a compelling summary narrative of actions, timelines and resource needs, is your Remarkability Agenda—it is a plan on a page that is backed up by extensive data, research and conversations. This plan identifies priorities, sequencing, resource needs, general project parameters and accountability. This matrix will be the backbone of the work you do to achieve remarkability.

The sequence laid out in the following chapters is the preferred sequence; moving through Purpose, People, then Platform generally builds from a foundation (Purpose) and expands to address more specific aspects of an organization (People and Platform), therefore the more that the transformation can follow that sequence the better. Some organizations may have such toxic relationships that People might be the first thing to be addressed. Others may have significant financial challenges, and that will rise to the top of the list.

The important thing to remember is that true remarkability cannot occur unless an organization is operating strongly and effectively in each of these organizational areas. Therefore, do not dismiss any area; examine each, prioritize changes, and get to work.

Now that you have done the work to build your Agenda, you must sell it and implement it. You will no doubt have to gain approval for this Agenda—likely through your board of directors—and then gain buy in with staff, and then implement by embedding it within strategies, plans and budgets. The following sections cover each of those next phases to achieving remarkability.

Gaining Approval

Most people wanting to implement their Remarkability Agenda will require some form of approval to proceed – from a board of directors, advisors, investors or others. This is where you will have to sell your plan to the decision makers in a compelling and thoughtful way. Through the assessment process you will have gleaned great information and data. You have built your Agenda outlining what needs to be done, when, by whom and have identified the estimated resources required.

But you can't just hand that to your board and expect an approval. This will need more. You will need the Remarkability Agenda matrix and summary but also key narrative and information components that will help to get your board, or approving body, onto the page of change that you need them to be on.

Before I outline the key steps to gaining approval, there are several key success factors you should follow to create the best chances of a resounding yes in your request for approval.

Key Success Factors to Change

Change is a tricky thing, particularly because it involves people. Any time something involves people and their emotions or sense of security and stability, immediately add a 10x complexity factor to the project.

As I've mentioned before, in the seven years that I was CEO, not one piece of the organization was left untouched. That's a lot of change. Not all of it was easy, but most of it was approved. In fact, I can count on one hand the number of times that a change proposed to our board was not approved.

When I discuss the range and scope of changes that we made at the Calgary Chamber, many people are amazed at what we were able to pull off. They view it as remarkable. They are surprised by the amount of change that has taken place. But more specifically, many are curious about how I was successful in getting change agreed to by my board, supported by staff, and successfully implemented as a team. That's because the approval and buy-in for change can often be as daunting and difficult as the change itself.

I acknowledge that I was tremendously fortunate to have had support for the changes I made at the Calgary Chamber. My board and colleagues were always very encouraging of the transformations that I wanted to bring about and gave me a lot of runway and benefit of the doubt. I know that will not be the case for every organization and leader.

Every time I needed support and approval, I made sure these key success factors were in place:

1. Ensure that your trust reservoir (I will discuss what this is in Chapter 7) with your board and colleagues is high. Attempting to ask for change approval, investments or transformation when your trust is running low with your board will often result in a no.

2. Identify supporters or allies and begin to plant the seeds of change through discussions and engagement – essentially "priming the pump."

3. Work with your board and leadership ahead of time to make sure people are thinking at the right level and have the right focus going into approval decisions. Nothing will get approved if you are talking big picture about the future when people are stuck in the weeds today.

4. Have good data to back up your case. This includes quantitative data that can demonstrate the need, opportunities and costs, as well as qualitative data that is from other sources or engagement with staff and customers.

5. Always be prepared to support someone in their questioning or concern for change. Keep in mind that you have been the architect of the Agenda or change proposal and have had a lot more time to consider it and understand it. Not everyone will be operating from that same place of knowledge and comfort. They will need time to understand it and to see all sides of it, including where they fit in.

Approval Request Components

Once you have all the key success factors in the best shape possible, convincing your board or other approving body to provide you with the mandate and resources to implement your Agenda can be achieved by following four steps: paint the picture, rationalize the change, outline the consequences of no change, and map the change. I illustrate each step with one of the biggest changes that I made during my tenure at the Calgary Chamber: the sale of our building.

Paint the Picture

Those being asked to support or approve a change need to know why a change is needed. You will need to paint a picture of the change so that people can visualize the end state, what the world will be like once the change has been completed. It's also necessary to articulate why things will be better because of the change, and to enable people to visualize themselves and/or the organization operating successfully within that vision. People need to see that life or performance will be better, or that there is in fact a place for them once the change is completed. Otherwise, they will be unlikely to support the change.

The sale of our building was a significant change for the organization. It had been our home for 32 years and was part of what people conceived of as the organization's identity. But it was old, costly, and didn't fit our brand or core business. My predecessors had looked at a variety of options: sell, renovate, status quo. I also looked at all the options and, after extensive consultation and analysis, I decided that we needed to sell the building.

Some members didn't want us to sell the building and were very vocal and active in trying to stop this decision. Some board members didn't want to sell the building. It was true that some staff would lose their jobs because selling meant the closure of our food and beverage operations. I had to paint the picture of why our organization would be better off without the building.

I created a narrative that spoke to the freedom to focus on our core business and our members. I talked about the financial freedom and flexibility we would have without having to dedicate resources to building systems. I articulated the amazing organizational advancements we could invest in with the sale proceeds. I tried to show how people's jobs would be

more focused, enjoyable, productive and meaningful—
ultimately creating better results and impact. Most people
understood this, yet some still hung on to the image of the
Chamber as a piece of real estate.

You aren't going to convince everyone.

Rationalize the Change

It is important people feel the need for the change, so you must
convincingly identify what's not working well, what requires
improving, and what opportunities are being missed. Be sure to
engage with affected parties or beneficiaries so that those
approving the change will see that you have been consultative
and have assessed options and impacts and risks associated
with the change.

Using data, stories and visuals to help rationalize the change is
important here. Include your assessment summary matrix to
demonstrate that you have done your due diligence and have
rigor behind your proposal. Supporting the rationale with solid
and detailed data, such as that gleaned in the analyses
discussed earlier in this chapter, is essential, as it shows that
you have done your homework and assessed the options and a
host of variables.

Even better than showing people data, or describing for them to
need for change, is to give them experiences that enable them
to actually feel the need for change. As an example, if there is a
need for change to a technology system, or a user experience,
put your board, and later your staff, through what your
customer or member experiences to illustrate the need for the
change. They will feel for themselves, firsthand, the difficulties
or problems with the current approach, and through a lived

experience of frustration or impediment, their likelihood of support should increase substantially.

To support the rationale for our building sale, I produced years' worth of financial data on what it cost us to operate the building. I showed that the financial picture could be so much brighter if we didn't have the building – the investments, the technological improvements, etc. I articulated how we had fallen behind as an organization because we spent time and money on running a building and restaurant, and not on being a chamber of commerce committed to helping our members and their businesses. I engaged with people who were resistant to the change and shared with them this information and the picture I had painted. Over time, I made my rounds to staff, board, members and stakeholders to provide them with data, insights and narrative as to why the time had come to sell the building.

Outline the Consequences of No Change

Too often, people rely on the case for change from the standpoint of the benefit of change. The reality is that an equally persuasive approach is to articulate the impacts or costs of *not* changing. What will be the lost opportunities, the lost revenue, the lost customers, the lost staff, or the lost productivity of not changing? Will you lose competitive position? Will some other organization come in and make the change, relegating you to irrelevance or mediocrity? Will this hamper your ability to make further changes that will position your organization for success? While some may feel this is using scare tactics or veiled threats, I disagree. No decision on change should be made without understanding the consequences of inaction or indecision. Without such consideration, any decision is being made from only one side of the equation.

As part of my data analysis for rationalizing the change, I created some forecasts for what the Chamber faced should we continue to hold on to the building. It showed increased costs going into an aging property. It showed potential options for us to renovate, including portions of our budget that would be going towards debt service. I also showed the continued lack of focus on the value proposition as our time was split between facility and members. I built a clear and compelling case, with both quantitative and qualitative information, for what life would be like if we remained owners of our building.

Map the Change

The vision or end state that you have articulated is usually exciting, dynamic, different and just what the doctor ordered. But it may be so different from the present situation that the magnitude of change scares, intimidates or turns people off. You may need to break it down for them and map it out. As one of my mentors reminds me, "you can't jump a canyon in one leap." People need to have the change broken down for them so that the jump is in fact many smaller jumps that seem easier and more achievable. People can be more comfortable with a series of smaller changes. Mapping this change creates the components of how you will tackle the change from an implementation or action plan standpoint.

As part of the proposal to sell the building, I created a plan that broke the change down into distinct phases: staff communication, engagement and support; member and stakeholder communication; public announcement; building marketing and sale; new space selection and design; move; and integration. I included as much detail as I could about what each phase would be like so that people could get a sense of the activities, what their role was, and when they could expect each phase to roll out. This provided clarity on the change that I was proposing.

The day of the board decision came. I presented the case for the sale. There was vigorous discussion and debate as to what the organization should do. Keep or sell? What will members think? What will we do with the funds? What will our new real estate costs be? Most board members agreed with me, and in the end, the motion to sell the building passed—but not unanimously.

Implementing the Remarkability Agenda

Once you have gained approval from your board or other body, you must now embark on implementation. The first step of any implementation is to introduce this change to your staff and colleagues so that they can buy in and be part of the transformation.

It is important that you build sufficient time for this first step of implementation to enable staff to understand the proposed changes, absorb them and then reflect so that they can ask questions and see how they may be able to help. You should never attempt to announce a big set of changes that will start implementation immediately, or heaven forbid, that staff should ever hear about major change from someone other than the leader of the organization. You want people to feel positive and supportive of the change, and so you should spend the time to set that up for success.

Change is hard. In their 2010 book *Switch: How to Change Things When Change is Hard*, Dan and Chip Heath suggest that change is often difficult because we fail to recognize that we have two opposing forces inside each of us—a rider and an elephant, one of whom is keen on the change (rider), and one who is resistant to it (elephant). Most approval and change processes do not actively plan for both. The approach to implementation discussed below incorporates the needs and views of both those supportive of, and potentially resistant to, change.

Gaining support, buy-in and excitement for the implementation of the Agenda should follow the same four-step process as outlined for approval but oriented to the team as opposed to the decision-making body. Staff need to have the picture painted for them about how life will be better once the Agenda is implemented and you have transformed—they need to see themselves reflected in that better place in ways that make them feel valued and meaningful in the overall scheme of things. They need to understand why the change is happening in terms of the missed opportunities and the continued struggles of the status quo. They need to understand the consequences of the status quo—such as job cuts, reduced budgets for salaries or development, or a challenged workplace. Finally, they need to understand the steps and sequencing of the change to gain an appreciation for what this means in terms of how and when it will impact them.

Sharing all that information in a personal and open environment is critical. Give people the time to absorb and reflect. Do it in a way that enables discussion and open conversation—for these are the folks that it will impact the most. Once you have delivered the information outlined above to your team, ensure that you reinforce the change and over-communicate. I use the roll out to the staff of the building sale as illustration.

Reinforce the Change

Reinforcing the change can be as simple as being positive about the change in all your communications and discussions. You'll also need to ensure that those that are on board and supportive of the change are vocal in their support so that they can help spread the optimism for the change. Advocates and supporters need to rally to ensure the change is approved and that it is successfully implemented.

As time went on, after we had communicated the building sale to the team, they became accustomed to the notion of the change. I worked hard to secure the vocal support of people both inside and outside the organization. I also worked to involve people in the change by bringing together a building committee, which engaged staff in helping select and design the new space and prepare for the move. This committee was also responsible for finding ways to make the transition to our new home as easy as possible.

Communicate, Communicate, Communicate

One classic reason why change initiatives do not gain buy-in and support along the way is that too many leaders forget, once they get approval for their change and announce it to the world, to keep people involved and up-to-date with the change process. I know I have been guilty of that myself and have learned from my mistakes. Board, staff and customers/members will need to have regular updates on how the change process is going, where it is along its path, and when completion can be expected. Err on the side of over-communicating versus under-communicating.

I kept the team updated on a regular basis, with emails and staff discussion on the topic at least once a week. The topic was a standing agenda item on our weekly leadership team meeting and our monthly all-staff meeting, and I provided email updates to staff approximately every two weeks. We shared information such as potential locations and designs—and preferred coffee vendors. My door was always open to discuss the change, and I actively sought out conversations with people who I knew had concerns. Actively communicating is key. As the leader, you may be sick of doing so, but never underestimate people's thirst for current information.

Not everyone will support or buy in. You will have to assess whether you have done enough to try and bring them onside, whether they will shift to a position of support over time, or whether they will be a challenge and obstacle to the change you propose in the Agenda. Depending on your assessment there are a range of options as to how to best deal with colleagues like this, and later in this chapter, I discuss ways to tackle some of the barriers to change.

Hopefully through this process you have achieved buy-in and support from most of your team. If this is the case, then it is time to start implementing your Remarkability Agenda. The Agenda comes to life by making it real—incorporating it into organizational strategies, annual plans and budgets. Then, it is time to get to work and start implementing the exciting things that are outlined in the following chapters—on everything from your brand and purpose, to culture, team and technology. The chapters that follow will outline exactly what you need to do to achieve remarkability for each element. Now the fun begins!

One comical anecdote about our building sale and move:

As the leadership team discussed our announcement to the staff, I thought long and hard about the people who would make the move to the new facility and what they would be most concerned about. I thought for a moment and it hit me. Coffee.

Given that we had our own coffee shop on the main floor, they would be most concerned about where they would get their coffee.

The day of the staff announcement came, and we brought everyone together and shared the news. I looked around the room and observed people's reactions. There were clearly some stunned people, so I let them have a moment to process this big change. I asked if anyone had any questions about the change or the move. A hand went up: "What are we going to do about the coffee?" Fortunately, we had planned for this and committed to a process to enable staff to pick the new coffee supplier. People are interesting—no matter how big the change is, they want to know how it is rooted in their daily lives and what will it mean for them. Clearly, coffee is one of a human's most basic and important needs.

Barriers to Change and Remarkability

Not everyone will be excited about change. You have been brought on to make things better, but there will likely be some people or existing structures that will make that change difficult.

Recall in Chapter 2 where we discussed what you will face as a new leader and the resistance that you should expect to encounter. Some people are nervous about the change you have been tasked to bring about because it might threaten their jobs, security and livelihoods. Others may not see their entire job at risk but are resistant to change and therefore will have a difficult time not only understanding the rationale for change but the change itself. Finally, there are others who simply will not want you to succeed.

While people may be the largest and most complex barrier to transformation, another invisible barrier exists. It is "the immune system," as discussed by Salim Ismail in *Exponential Organizations: Why new organizations are ten times better, faster, and cheaper than yours (and what to do about it)*[3].

The immune system is the established way of doing things. People, culture, policies, procedures, rules (written and unwritten), worldviews, attitudes, egos, structure, invested capital, geographic distribution, and much more. It is a series of established ways, means and mindsets designed to protect the organization by minimizing change and risk. It is the way that things are currently done, and it creates organizational resistance to change. A new CEO will have to assess the state of their organization's immune system to determine where the transformation might be most difficult, and what tactics might be needed to address certain changes over others to increase the chances of success.

Often companies get around the immune system by embarking on change, innovation and transformation at the edge of the organization—something like a Google X team or skunkworks initiative. Getting around the immune system will depend on the organization. If people are excited for, supportive of, and willing to undergo change, it will be easier. As the organizational leader, you do have some latitude to create the space for breaking rules and other existing parts of the immune system to help with change success. If there are things like policies, rules, procedures or systems standing in the way of change that you can eliminate or suspend—do it!

Inevitably, some challenge or difficulty will come from your board. They won't see the need to change or transform. Or the move to a more governance-based, high-performing board isn't what they want it to be, because they want to take on their pet project or become famous from their board role. Chapter 7 of this book, on the board of directors, gives you some tangible ideas of how to get your board onside, if the process used here is not effective. As the leader of the organization, you will have to assess whether you can effect change with some effort, or whether it is a lost cause, in which case you will need to evaluate your options. But it must be stressed that becoming remarkable is highly contingent upon your board supporting and approving the Remarkability Agenda you create. You will have a difficult time getting support for your Agenda if you have the wrong people on your board, or if they are there for the wrong reasons.

Finally, you will likely read this book and at points say to yourself "we can't do this" or "I don't have the time or resources to accomplish this." I recognize that there is a lot to a Remarkability Agenda. You may not be a big organization. You may not have a big staff. You may not have a big budget. You may not have the time. That is okay.

Remarkability, as laid out in this book, reflects the preferred and optimal state. The key is: work on what you can, following the sequence I've laid out, and make the transformations that you can. Even small advancements or adjustments can make a difference. Don't despair if you can't do it all or feel like this is just too much for your smaller organization. Do what you can. Chip away. Remarkability isn't about size or budget. It is about mindset and discipline and drive.

Resource Kit

Ask This

- Is now the right time to undertake an assessment of the organization?
- Do I have all the information I need to be able to assess my organization?
- Do I have good data and analysis to work from?
- Is the board on side for me to begin digging into the organization and unearthing some potentially less-than-positive findings?
- Will I be able to assemble a sufficient group of people to provide candid and meaningful feedback?
- What major areas of the three pillars need attention?
- Do I think that this organization is ready for this kind of change?
- Do I think that the board will approve and that others will buy in to the need for change?
- Can I craft an effective and compelling Remarkability Agenda?
- What kind of immune system exists in my organization? How might I address it or counter-act it?

Do This to be Remarkable

- Complete your big-picture assessment and identify trends, themes and focus areas.
- Complete the eight diagnostic assessments.
- Complete the summary assessment matrix template.
- Evaluate options and priorities and create your Remarkability Agenda.
- Gain approval and staff buy-in for implementation.

Review This

- BOOKS
  - Dan and Chip Heath, *Switch: How to Change Things When Change is Hard*. Crown Business (2010).
  - Dan and Chip Heath, *Made to Stick: Why some Ideas Survive and Others Die*. Random House (2007).
  - Salim Ismail, *Exponential Organizations: Why new organizations are ten times better, faster, and cheaper than yours (and what to do about it)*. Diversion Books (2014).
  - Chris Ertel and Lisa Kay Salomon, *Moments of Impact: How to Design Strategic Conversations That Accelerate Change*. Simon & Schuster (2014).
  - Alexander Osterwalder and Yves Pigneur, *Business Model Generation*. John Wiley and Sons Inc. (2010).

- OTHER
  - "How to Beat the Transformation Odds" McKinsey and Company: https://www.mckinsey.com/business-functions/organization/our-insights/how-to-beat-the-transformation-odds
  - Resources on benchmark studies or financial and organizational analyses from organizations like:
    - American Society of Association Executives www.asaecenter.org
    - American Institute of CPAs www.aicpa.org
    - CPA Canada www.cpacanada.ca
    - Institute of Corporate Directors www.icd.ca
    - National Association of Corporate Directors www.nacdonline.org

PART 2: The Three Pillars of Remarkability

PURPOSE

Your purpose is your reason for being. It is why you exist and what you aim to achieve in the world. It is your long-term aspiration, commitment and vision. Your purpose forms the basis of the values that you hold true, and the culture those values form.

The Purpose pillar is comprised of two elements:

- Your Brand and Your Why
- Your Culture and Values

Let's look at each one in turn.

CHAPTER 5: Purpose: Your Brand and Your Why

What is it?	Your brand is your reputation. It is who you are, what you stand for, and what all your decisions and actions should be based on. It is the promises you make and your organizational personality. Your purpose is why your organization exists; the contribution and impact you want to have for your customer or member. It is also the value your customers get and the true reason they engage with you.
Why is it important?	It creates the foundation and focus for your entire organization—business model, value proposition, people and infrastructure.
Where do you start?	• Undertake a brand audit and assess the health of the brand. • Determine if you need to rebrand or just better activate your existing brand. • Explore the historical origins of the organization and past purpose statements. • Convene discussion on what the new purpose should be.
Remarkable is:	• A clear, inspiring and compelling brand position, including purpose/why statement, values, personality and story • A brand and purpose that is lived every day by staff and implemented through all that the organization is and does

"Your brand is what people say about you when you're not in the room." Jeff Bezos[4]

When I arrived at the Calgary Chamber, the board had recently launched a study that was meant to look at potential growth markets for new members. After some time, the consultant returned to the board, not with the expected finished product, but with this: "You have a brand problem."

When I started, the community, members and stakeholders were telling us that they didn't know what the Chamber was any more. They didn't know what it stood for or who it served. They didn't know why it existed. In 2010, the Calgary economy was firing on all cylinders—it had been the fastest growing economy in Canada for over a decade, with a growing corps of young dynamic entrepreneurs—but the Calgary Chamber just didn't reflect what was happening in Calgary at that time. In fact, it did the opposite.

People said that the Chamber felt like an old boys' club: pale, male and stale. Our building featured a lot of dark wood, and our events were populated by lots of men in suits, with an over-emphasis on political speakers. Events were not exciting. The only people under 40 at our events or on our membership rolls were there because they were given a ticket, were trying to network for a better job, or had an interest in policy and advocacy. We were labelled as outdated.

I was brought in to change that. My mandate was clear: change this place into something more vibrant, fresh, younger and reflective of Calgary's dynamic business community. I was brought in to fix the brand.

Clearly, that had to start with our purpose.

But, before we get too far down the path of purpose, let's look at brand overall in some more detail, for purpose is an essential part of a brand.

What is Brand?

Your brand is your reputation. It is your commitment to your customer or member. It is the living embodiment of your purpose, values, traits, and characteristics of who you are as an organization. You live your brand with every decision you make, every event you hold and every person you hire. Every interaction must reflect your brand.

Brands are funny things. So many people think it is your logo, or your tag line. But a brand is much more than that. It is you and your promise to your customer or member.

A brand is not a logo. A brand is not a colour scheme. It is not a slogan or key messages. A brand is not an empty promise or a statement that can't be backed up. It is the organization's personality and its promise to its customer.

A brand platform has many elements, including:

- Purpose
- Promise
- Values
- Personality traits
- Story
- Visual, physical, experiential and auditory elements that reflect the platform

The core of a brand is the purpose, or why you exist.

The Brand Challenge: You Have One Whether You Like It or Not

The interesting thing about brands is that you have one whether you like it or not, just like a reputation. In the absence of creating a clear and well-managed brand like that of Coca Cola, Apple or Four Seasons, your brand gets decided for you by your customers, competitors, stakeholders or the community.

The challenge that the Calgary Chamber faced was that no one there really knew much about brand and how to manage it, therefore it had ultimately been abandoned. Through the passage of time and the host of decisions made about what the Chamber did, how it spoke, the experiences at events and much more, the customer and the community had assigned the Chamber a brand—and that brand was old and stale.

There were previous attempts to change the brand, but they were all made with the belief that your brand was just the slogan, key messages, or a marketing campaign. In other words, those who attempted to change the "brand" approached it as a façade or what was communicated externally. They didn't understand that the brand is an organization's DNA and that you can't change your brand by simply stating how you'd like to be perceived. If only it were that easy. You must become what you want to be perceived as being.

Chambers, associations and other member-based organizations across North America, and in fact around the world, face this brand challenge. Many of these organizations could be described as old and stale. Why? Because they have neglected their purpose and their brand.

They have missed the changes happening around them and they have failed to develop a compelling value proposition around the current and emergent needs of their target market. They have failed to evolve and adapt. They have believed that what has always worked will continue to work, and that has been reflected in the way they present themselves and their offering. And so, their brand has been impacted negatively and often through the chatter that happens beyond their control and within the community. They have simply failed to recognize that brands require constant nurturing.

Many organizations have launched into a "rebranding" initiative only to have the outcome be a new logo, new colour palette, new cutlery, new tag line, new drapes or a new event. None of these things are a rebranding. They are paint over the rust. In the long run, they will do little to ensure the organization's survival, and they will not make an organization remarkable. Remarkability will come only from a sincere and deep reflection on, and redevelopment of, an organization's brand and purpose.

I am reminded of "The Brady Bunch Movie," a spoof of the original television series of the 1970s. In the film, set in 1995, the Bradys still exist like it is the 1970s and, not surprisingly, encounter a lot of problems. The father, an architect, can't sell his designs because everything he does, including a gas station, looks like the Brady house. Too many organizations are living like the Bradys—thinking that the world doesn't change, what they offer today will always be wanted, or that a little colour here or there on the same old design will convince people that a meaningful change has occurred.

People aren't that stupid. They expect a lot more from you and need to see a good reason for why you exist. You need to be continually reinforcing with your target market why they should pick you and your brand over another.

Organizations around the world (like chambers, associations, service clubs, even golf clubs) have not managed their brands and have lost their value proposition. They are therefore handed a brand by their constituents, or worse, former constituents, of irrelevance. The brand labels given by the community have a high degree of stickiness to them, and it takes a lot to change people's minds to something different. While we did it at the Calgary Chamber, it took a lot of time and effort. If you can avoid getting to the point where you're handed a negative brand perception, I highly recommend it. It is remarkable how much hard work it takes to develop and maintain a positive brand, but how easy it is to be given a negative one. Like the old saying goes about a reputation: it takes a lifetime to earn, and a moment to destroy.

That is why a new CEO needs to get a firm assessment of the state and health of their organizational brand, and if it is in bad shape, take steps to fix it.

There are many things that a new CEO can spend money on. Hiring a proper brand consultant is one of those expenses that will pay dividends down the road. Don't skimp or think that your internal communications person can do it. A true brand professional will take you through the whole audit and brand process, resulting in a true rebrand of your organization, including your purpose and how the brand should be communicated, lived and activated within the organization. Hire the best that you can afford.

At the Calgary Chamber, we underwent an entire rebranding effort. We hired a firm to help us with our rebranding. They took us back to our core and looked at our history, our goals, our desired traits and impacts. They talked to staff, members, former members, stakeholders and the community about what the chamber was, is and could be. Through this process, they created a strong brand platform, including a refreshed and clear purpose, that still exists today.

As part of our branding exercise we developed a new purpose—our why statement. Ours became: To help make our member's business more successful. This framed our brand and everything that we did. Looking back, I don't think it was inspirational enough; while it did address the problem, our members faced (business success), it could have been more aspirational and better connected to the needs, emotions and desires of our members. If I could go back in time and do it again, I would have made it bigger and bolder. At the time it resonated as practical and what people needed. But now, after righting the ship, it deserves something more inspirational.

Brand Audit: This Might Sting a Bit

The place to start in assessing a brand is with a brand audit. Most brand strategists can provide this service either independently or as part of an overall rebrand effort. A brand audit will examine internal topics such as the way a brand is presented, from the look and feel, tone of voice or story and the experiences that are provided. Externally, the audit will look at things like:

- Brand perception: what your audience thinks about you
- Brand expectations: the gap between what your audience wants versus what they are getting from you
- Brand value: the true value your audience could get from you versus what you do

You first need to know where you stand in order to know what you need to fix. This type of audit is impossible to do internally. You need the distance and impartiality of an external advisor or consultant.

What you uncover can be a hard pill to swallow but a necessary one if you are to truly address the problem.

(Re)Branding: That's Going to Leave a Mark

If you lack a formalized brand, or if your brand is in bad shape, as CEO you should invest in a rebrand project.

Again, to be clear, a rebrand is not just an exercise of changing some colour palettes or the logo. Too many organizations think they can either change the logo, redo their website, or use some on-trend words like "innovation" or "disruption" and suddenly that is a substitute for rebranding.

A rebranding is a deep dive process that explores values, characteristics, personality and commitment. It creates a purpose for your organization and makes a promise to your customer or member.

One caution, however: whatever brand purpose you select, you must be prepared to live by it. Your brand purpose must be something you live by and demonstrate constantly, especially when it would be so much easier, cheaper or faster not to do it.

With a new purpose, and a redeveloped brand, a leader now has the initial foundation of remarkability. The first of the three pillars must be in place for the other two—People and Platform—to be successful and stable. Using the refreshed

Calgary Chamber brand as a platform, we embarked on the rest of our transformation. Our refreshed purpose and brand helped articulate what the "new" Calgary Chamber was all about in terms of experience, offering, language and feel. We had set the foundations for remarkability.

We changed the way we talked about ourselves and backed it up with substance in terms of our offering, experience and people. We made a very conscious effort to not only say we were on a path to change but to live that change. We used our brand as our guide and our decision-making filter.

We used it to abandon certain events like our annual gala and 7:15 networking breakfasts. We used it to create new offerings like ONWARD (which will be discussed in more detail in Chapter 9 on value proposition) and Fast Growth Champions events aimed at entrepreneurs and innovation. We used it as the framework for our new membership model. We used it as a lens for determining what we should do or support. We changed our look and feel to reflect our brand and help us express it.

We had launched the refreshed brand at our AGM in 2012, articulating its purpose, personality, elements and characteristics. We had created a few new events that were focused on the future and on creativity and imagination. We had cancelled our annual fundraising dinner that felt like a blend of pocket picking and self-congratulations. Yet we were still in our old historic wood-paneled building. The new brand had not yet stuck.

The day it finally felt like the new brand had stuck was the day we moved into our new space, which had been designed using the brand's principles and was intended to focus on our members using space and technology. The final piece of the puzzle was the space, the physical embodiment of the new brand.

Rebrands take time. You need to not only roll out the change, but you also need to consistently back it up with value and experience that reflects that new brand. Because of the stickiness of a brand that exists in people's minds, it will take multiple consistent interactions with a new brand for someone to even contemplate changing their perception of the brand. It took us some time beyond the move into the new space before our members felt that our rebranding had taken hold.

Let's now do a deeper dive on the core of a brand and the foundational pillar of remarkability: purpose.

What is a Purpose?

Brand experts have been espousing forever the importance of having a strong purpose or reason for being. It creates part of a brand personality and profile to begin to build your organization around. But it wasn't really until we began to pay attention to a TEDx video[5] by Simon Sinek that the notion of a why, or a purpose, began to sink in.

Sinek's video illustrates his theory of the Golden Circle which is that every organization needs to be able to articulate their why, how and what. What makes his concept different, and better, is that an organization should start by defining their why, not their what. It is rooted in the notion that organizations will be more successful, and customers and members more drawn to you, if you define your reason for existence first, and then define the how and what of bringing that purpose to life.

A compelling purpose is meant to evoke a feeling, response, emotion and connection between the organization and those who it attracts as employees, customers and advocates. It is meant to rally people, provide something bigger to shoot for and to hold on to, and to create engagement, better decisions and long-term performance. Think of a compelling purpose as a competitive advantage, a recruitment and retention tool and a business growth engine all in one.

Building any organization by starting with a clear and compelling purpose is essential. Brand specialists around the world speak passionately about the need to define an organizational purpose as part of the brand. A strong organization can't be built if it really doesn't know why it exists or the impact that it wants to have on its customers, members or the world.

So, what is a good purpose statement? It is essentially why an organization exists and the challenges that it is aiming to solve and/or the impact that it wants to have. It is inspirational, aspirational and long-term in orientation. A good purpose is about the impact and contribution that you want to have with your customers or members, and the world. It should generate a passion in customers, members and employees because of its aspirational nature.

Why No Purpose?

Many organizations are currently struggling, and on the verge of disappearing, because for decades they have built uninspiring mission statements about *what* they do and have utterly forgotten *why* they do what they do. Many chambers define themselves as delivering advocacy, events and networking. Associations define themselves as representing the profession or movement. That is what they do, not why they do it. And that's why they've lost people to other more inspiring entities, activities, pursuits and investments.

Why do so many organizations find themselves in this position? The origins of the "mission statement" are murky, but since the 1980s, this idea that it's important to tell customers what an organization does caught on like wildfire, and organizational retreats and strategy sessions were built around the mind-numbing experience of collectively defining a mission statement using vague, generic and uninspiring language. And so began the decline in the connection between organization and its reason for being.

I'm sure that at some point in our careers we've all had to sit in a room thinking up mission statements. And we all know that they don't work. One of the reasons they don't work is because they tend to be meaningless and robotic statements that include some variety or combination of words like "strive," "achieve," "deliver," "innovative," "responsive," "value," "diversity," and "sustainably." Few of them are compelling. Few of them are unique and even fewer of them are remarkable. In fact, the large majority of them are highly unremarkable and do not serve to do anything other than adorn some office wall somewhere. Employees don't remember them, and customers aren't moved by them. If this is the reality, what is the point of traditional mission statements?

There isn't one.

When I arrived at the Calgary Chamber, there was no purpose statement, but there *was* a mission statement: "We are the pre-eminent business organization in Calgary, representing the voice of business, valuing its diversity."

This kind of statement doesn't sell memberships. It's not how you'll respond when someone asks you what your organization does. It's not something that will get a top recruit to sign the offer. Such a statement is just like the hundreds of thousands of statements that have been developed over decades by organizations thinking that it was the right thing to do. And we have all paid the price in terms of decreased connection, decreased customer loyalty and increased apathy.

The good news is that we now understand psychology, buying behaviour, and demographics much better than we used to. Replacing mission statements with powerful purpose statements that get backed up through implementation of brand, products and service offerings and experiences creates the platform for remarkability. Staff will remember a powerful purpose and will be motivated by it. Customers and members will feel an affinity, and communities will be created.

Why the Why? Why is a Purpose Important?

We've just covered what a purpose is and some of the challenges that organizations have faced because of focusing for too long on the what instead of the why. To create remarkability, you need to put the why *before* the what.

A clear and compelling purpose is the foundation, the bedrock, of any remarkable organization. Once established, it becomes the lens through which you make all your decisions as a leader and organization. If faced with challenges, choices or struggles, you ask: Does this align to our purpose? Is this in keeping with our purpose? Will this advance our purpose? As the leader of the organization, you will need to be evangelical about its adoption and infiltration into all parts of the organization. You will need to make sure it makes its way into every nook and cranny, and that people embrace it, live it and nurture it.

A leader cannot build a team without a clear sense of purpose. A board cannot govern without a clear purpose. A business model and value proposition cannot be built without a clear purpose. A strategy cannot be framed without a clear purpose. And key infrastructure needs like technology and facilities certainly cannot be determined without a clear purpose.

The purpose creates the foundation upon which you build a business model, value proposition, strategy and operation, and thereby secure and retain your customers and members. You can't begin to offer something of value without understanding first why you are doing it, and the value or contribution you are providing to your customer or member.

While the struggles and challenges being faced by many organizations are diagnosed as problems with their value proposition or membership model, the reality is that if the purpose is not clearly defined then they are likely not building the right value proposition or member model. They are then making poor choices and losing customers and members. What is deemed to be a value proposition issue has deeper roots. The purpose is at the core and the base of so much for any organization.

A clear and compelling purpose is also essential for attracting and retaining talent. Purpose happens to be one of the three critical things that motivates humans to do what they do, according to Daniel Pink in *Drive: The Surprising Truth About What Motivates Us*. According to Pink, people seek to be part of something greater than themselves and to make a meaningful contribution within that structure. Along with mastery and autonomy, people are intrinsically motivated by a purpose. An organization that can find, and hold on to, people whose purpose aligns with the organization's purpose will, assuming they have opportunities for mastery and autonomy, have a huge advantage in terms of attracting and retaining top talent.

In *Good is the New Cool: Market Like You Give a Damn*, Afdhel Aziz and Bobby Jones suggest that organizations need to develop an impactful purpose to help attract and retain millennial talent. Millennials (born 1981-1997) want to work for an organization that has a larger purpose and is making a difference in their community or the world. They are attracted by organizations that not only define, but also live, a meaningful purpose. If you want to attract the top millennial talent, either within your organization or even as contractors, you'll need to build a solid purpose.

Along the lines of creating a solid purpose to attract customers, members and staff, I have been quite impressed by the brands of the chambers in Orlando, Florida, Des Moines, Iowa, and Indianapolis, Indiana. They are dynamic and convey a highly energetic place to work and do business, as all are growing as hot spots for innovation, technology and advanced manufacturing. I also see great international brand building with the chambers in Vancouver, B.C, Edmonton, Alberta, Toronto, Ontario, Winnipeg, Manitoba, Halifax, Nova Scotia, and Montreal, Quebec. With their affiliations to the World Trade Centre and related international efforts, they all speak to an international and trade element that works to create bridges for their business communities to other locations outside their cities and countries. All these chambers, in the United States and Canada, then back up the brand with supporting programs that bring the brand to life. Building a strong brand that represents who you are and what you commit to your customer can differentiate you from the pack.

The need for a compelling purpose should at this point be clear. It's about creating your foundation and creating connection to your customers/members and your team. The imperative of any new leader, or a leader tasked with transformation, is to define a compelling purpose. In the absence of that, the rest of any transformation, and working to create remarkability, will fall flat. Let's look at how to define your purpose.

How to Define Your Purpose

Establishing a compelling purpose is simple but it's not easy. Engaging your team, customers or members, and stakeholders, ask these basic questions:

1. Why does this organization exist?
2. Why do this work?
3. What problem are we here to solve?
4. What do we really care about?
5. What do we believe in or stand for?
6. When have you been most proud of this organization?
7. What is this organization's contribution or true value that we provide?
8. What impact has this organization had on you?
9. What is the one thing that we can hope to accomplish as an organization?

Simple, right? Where it gets hard is that there are no quick answers to these questions. As a leader it will take you time to answer these questions thoughtfully and deeply.

Often, impactful purpose statements are created by the founder and have origins with the beginnings of the organization. If you are not the founder, then it is up to you to explore any historical why/purpose of the organization, and assess its relevance, meaning and adoption in today's context.

If you need to start from the beginning, this process is best conducted by a person experienced with brand, and as part of an overall (re)branding effort. Many brand strategists are experts in being able to craft an impactful and meaningful purpose statement for an organization. Make sure you stay away from jargon and meaningless words that will sound much like your mission statement.

If you can't have this done by a brand strategist, you can follow a process like that mapped out by Simon Sinek in *Find Your Why*[6], such as:

1. Gather stories through stakeholder interviews and workshops and share them.
2. Identify themes among the stories and examples.
3. Draft and refine your why statement, that is aspirational and inspirational and addresses contribution and impact of the organization on the lives of customers, staff and community.

To bring your why to life, create a brand story about your organization, where you are going, what you hope to accomplish and what the end state, or success, looks like. Help people understand how your brand and purpose will have meaning in their lives.

Establishing a purpose that defines an organization's reason for existence and helps define its contribution and impact in the world will create longevity and depth to that organization. It is a journey of discovery, not invention. Often it is rooted in the beliefs of the founder and touches on the significance that the organization stands for in all that it does for the world.

It is clear that those organizations that develop and live a compelling purpose are those that are set on a trajectory to create movements and success. They are set up to become remarkable.

Resource Kit

Ask This—Diagnostic 1

(You can complete all diagnostic questions from each chapter online at www.makingremarkable.com)[7]
Use a rating of Yes=1, No=0. A score of 80% or better indicates that you are likely remarkable in that element.

1. Brand
   a. Does your organization have a formal brand platform, including purpose, values, personality, and guide on how it should be applied?
   b. Is your brand reflective of a remarkable organization? Is it aspirational and does it connect with your target market?
   c. Is someone in your organization tasked with overseeing the integrity and implementation of your brand?
   d. Does everyone in your organization know how to live by the brand in their interactions and work?
   e. Do you ensure that your brand is reflected in all your events, experiences, interactions, meetings and environments in all possible ways?

2. Purpose Currency and Quality
   a. Does your organization have a purpose or why statement (note, specifically a statement as to why you exist)?

b. Was your purpose written or reviewed within the past three years?

c. Is it inspirational, about the impact you want to have, or the value you want to deliver to your target market?

d. Is the statement focused and specific as to solving or addressing a specific need?

e. Do at least 80% of your customers/members believe you live up to your purpose/why (as gleaned through annual customer/member surveys)? (Mark No if you don't ask this question in your annual survey)

3. Organizational Activation and Staff Engagement

a. Is your purpose used as a means of assessing strategy, investments and new directions for the organization?

b. Is your purpose a means of defining your target market and therefore your value proposition?

c. Is your purpose embedded within the organization (e.g., published/displayed in strategic documents, office signage, website, meeting materials etc.)?

d. Is your purpose used as a filter for HR purposes such as hiring, firing and performance reviews?

e. Is your purpose known and lived by staff (i.e., can they recite it, and do they act in accordance with it)?

Do This to be Remarkable

- Shift mindset from brand as look, to brand as promise and reputation.
    - o Your brand is not your logo. Your brand is your promise, your personality and your DNA. It

must permeate all you are and do.

- Complete a brand audit.
  - This will assess whether your current brand is positive or negative, and whether you have the right approach in place to activate your brand.

- Hire a brand consultant.
  - This is not a communications or design exercise. This is a strategic exercise.

- Abandon the mission statement mindset.
  - Too many organizations are rooted in what they do versus why they do it. Focus on why you do what you do, and you will be set up for remarkability.

- Explore history.
  - Look at why the organization was started. Reflect on history and origins. Do research to understand why it all began.

- Engage your constituents.
  - Build an engagement process that involves everyone: board, staff and customers. If your purpose is going to be about helping your constituents solve problems, then constituents need to be part of it.

- Be bold.
  - Be inspirational, aspirational and emotional in what you want to state as your brand purpose. Don't put too many boundaries on what it is. Evoke emotion and engagement through aspiration and inspiration.

Review This

- BOOKS
  - Howard Schultz, *Onward: How Starbucks Fought for Its Life without Losing Its Soul.* Rodale (2011).
  - Simon Sinek, *Start with Why: How Great Leaders Inspire Everyone to Take Action.* Portfolio (2005).
  - Simon Sinek, *Find your Why: A Practical Guide for Discovering Purpose For You and Your Team.* Portfolio Penguin (2017).
  - Simon Sinek, *Leaders Eat Last: Why Some Teams Pull Together and Others Don't.* Portfolio/Penguin (2014).
  - Seth Godin, *Purple Cow: Transform your Business by Being Remarkable.* Penguin Books (2007).
  - Seth Godin, *All Marketers are Liars.* Portfolio (2005).
  - Afdhel Aziz and Bobby Jones, *Good is the New Cool: Market Like You Give a Damn.* Regan Arts (2016).
  - Daniel Pink, *Drive: The Surprising Truth About What Motivates Us.* Riverhead Books (2009).

- OTHER
  - Steve Jobs on the Apple brand: https://www.youtube.com/watch?v=TNYbcqyyj68
  - Simon Sinek talks about how great leaders inspire action: https://www.youtube.com/watch?v=u4ZoJKF_VuA
  - Marca Strategy podcast on brands and brand strategy: www.abrandedworldpodcast.com

CHAPTER 6: Purpose: Culture and Values

What is it?	Your culture is the sum of your values. They define what is important to the organization and how it will conduct itself. Your culture and your values define both how you operate and the dynamics amongst colleagues and customers or members.
Why is it important?	Your culture is more important than strategy. It is the force that powers everything that happens within your organization. Culture will make or break an organization's remarkability, and therefore should be a key part of hiring, firing and rewarding.
Where do you start?	• Determine features of your desired culture. • Assess the current culture against the desired state. • Develop a plan to adapt or change the culture.
Remarkable is:	• A meaningful and deeply held set of values that drives behaviours, processes and interactions • Bold and inspirational values that reflect the organization and go beyond bland and generic words • Highly activated values embedded within HR practices, with regular means of reinforcing the values, and recognition and rewards • Visibility of the values throughout the organization, both physically and virtually

"Culture eats strategy for breakfast." Peter Drucker[8]

I came to the Calgary Chamber having developed Calgary's economic development strategy. I was a strategy guy. To me, nothing trumped strategy. If you didn't have a strategy, nothing could work. But as I spent more time as a new CEO, it became clear that Drucker, a noted strategist himself, was right.

An organization's culture is its lifeblood. It dictates how people show up and perform every day. It is not simply the game rooms of Silicon Valley, or the boiler rooms of Wall Street. These things simply reflect culture. Culture, rather, is the aggregation of an organization's values. Culture is what you and people in the organization do when no one is looking. Its importance must not be understated for a culture can either enable, or disable, a transformation. Bad cultures will not create remarkable organizations. You will need a culture that fosters remarkability. And it needs to start with you.

The Importance of Culture and Values

If this culture thing eats strategy for breakfast, you know it's important. Nothing effective or meaningful can get done if the culture is not oriented around an organization's purpose and what it wants to achieve. Who gets hired, who stays, who leaves, how people show up and perform at their jobs—all of this is determined by the culture and is the ultimate determinant of what you will produce and how your organization will perform. And whether it will achieve remarkability.

With the growth in purpose-focused organizations, the alignment of a strong culture and values behind that purpose is ever more important. An organization will need to ensure it is congruent in terms of its purpose, its values and the people that it hires to reach its potential to be remarkable. Organizational purpose, culture, and values all roll up into an organizational brand. All of it must align for an organization to be successful and remarkable.

Do you want to find and keep the best people aligned to your purpose? Then make sure you have a strong set of values that you can embed within the processes of hiring, firing, and rewarding. A values-based approach to hiring and performance assessment is a rigorous and meaningful way to engage with employees, and results in alignment of purpose with passionate people who live up to the vision and approach outlined and modeled by the CEO. Yes that's right, it starts with you the leader. As talked about early in this book, you must model the way and set the example.

Understanding the Existing Culture

A new CEO will have gleaned insight into the existing culture from their organizational assessment. They will have had a chance to observe people in action and will have had a sufficient number of conversations to be able to understand what drives people, how people show up, what they value and what the operating system of the organization is like.

If a CEO wants to dig deeper, they should interview staff and ask them:

1. What words would you use to describe this organization?
2. What is the vibe and feel of this place?
3. What do you think are our values?
4. When we do our best work, how do we achieve that and what does it feel like?
5. What parts of this organization make you proud to be a part of it?
6. On your best day, what happened? On your worst day?

With a sense of what the existing culture is like, the new CEO needs to ask: What do I like? What do I want to keep? What don't I like? What do I want to change?

This understanding of the current culture should be matched up against a view of what the new CEO wants as their preferred or improved culture for the organization. This will help identify those things that will need to change, and the new values or elements that will replace the existing ones. For example, staff may not be very concerned about deadlines and commitments to each other, while the new CEO wants deadlines and accountability to be significant parts of an improved culture.

The Realities of a Culture Change

Many new CEOs come into an organization preaching the need to "build a better culture" or to "improve the culture" or "change the culture." While that may be the case, a new CEO must recognize a few important things:

1. A culture already exists. It may have been deliberately developed, or it may have simply settled in over time because of leaders, group actions, decisions, indecisions or other factors.

2. People hired before you arrived were hired to fit the existing culture. They generally fit that mold and continue to contribute to the culture that exists.

3. Espousing the need to change will get people asking, "What's wrong with our culture?" "If the new CEO wants to change our culture, what will that mean for me?" People will likely be concerned about their future place in the organization.

4. You cannot change culture unilaterally or instantaneously. It takes sound process, time, support,

buy-in or staffing changes. It is not always an easy or straightforward process.

To effectively and lastingly change the culture, the new CEO needs the support of existing staff. It's likely that not everyone will buy into a culture shift, but those that the CEO wishes to keep in the transformed organization will have to be persuaded of the need for an improved, or completely new, culture, and the process for arriving there.

Therefore, a new leader needs to talk about:

- Their vision for a new culture
- The challenges with the current culture
- Why the new culture will be better and what the end state will be like
- Why people will be better off in the new culture

Some staff will be excited about a culture shift, but others won't be. Some will come on board over time. Others will leave on their own, while some will need to be replaced because they're not living the values associated with the new culture. A new CEO needs to be prepared for all of this.

When I arrived at the Calgary Chamber there was a culture. It was a very cordial place. People treated each other well and there was little disruption in terms of work due to challenging relationships or conflict. They seemed like a close-knit bunch.

But it wasn't a high-performance culture, and performance, accountability, deadlines and excellence were not important to them. It was also very fragmented with no sense of collective team spirit and no unifying theme to the work they were doing. There were a lot of well-entrenched silos. Within a relatively short span of time, I saw the things that I wanted to preserve (good working relationships) and the things I wanted to change (the lack of a high-performance culture).

When to Change the Culture

At the Calgary Chamber, I began to shift culture informally by changing out some of the team and making different hiring decisions that better reflected the high-performance culture that I wanted to build. With these changes came people who were a better fit for my desired culture and team. They then made their own staffing choices that aligned with the values I hired them to embody. I implemented more intense performance management systems that focused on those aspects of a higher-performing culture that I wanted to bring in.

The time to purposefully embark on a culture change exercise depends on three things:

1. When you have a clear enough sense of what your desired culture and values look like on the other side of the process

2. When you feel you understand the existing culture sufficiently to know what you want to keep and what you want to change

3. When you have a sufficient critical mass of people on the team that you feel embody or represent the end-state culture that a change of values and culture can be successful

The timing for this will be different for each leader and organization.

How to Set or Change the Culture— Establish Your Values

Culture is about setting your values and living those values every day.

It starts with having a clearly defined purpose, which, based on the previous chapter, you should have defined. Next, you must be able to identify the core values that you wish to be reflected in the organization you're leading. Knowing this as a CEO or leader is vital to ensuring the process will be effective, as discussed below.

There are many ways to establish or refresh organizational values, but the one that worked at the Calgary Chamber is Jim Collins' Mars group values exercise[9].

The approach that Collins suggests is to imagine you've been asked to recreate the best aspects of your organization on Mars, but the rocket ship seats a maximum of seven people. Choose five to seven people on the team who reflect your core values or desired values for the organization, are well respected by their colleagues, and have a high level of competence in their roles. This group will be asked to help shape the values of the organization as a team over a period of a few weeks.

The team will be crafting three components of the values:

1. The values statements – no more than four

2. A narrative for each value statement

3. Keywords that define what each value statement includes in terms of how individuals are expected to behave

This "Mars group" should convene, facilitated by a third party, and should start by wrestling with the following questions, as framed by Jim Collins[10]:

1. What core values do you bring to work, values so fundamental that you hold them regardless of whether they are rewarded?

2. How would you describe to your loved ones the core values that you stand for in your work and that you hope they stand for in their working lives?

3. If you awoke tomorrow with enough money to retire, would you continue to hold on to these core values?

4. Can you envision these values being as valid 100 years from now as they are today? Would you want the organization to continue to hold these values, even if at some point one or more of them became a competitive disadvantage?

5. If you were to start a new organization tomorrow in a different line of work, what core values would you build into the new organization?

The answers to these questions will generate a series of words, statements and stories that reflect the dynamic aspects of the organization that people hold dear as individuals and colleagues. This list of words and statements serves as a starting point for the creation of values.

The next step is to group the words into some common themes from which the value statements can be developed. Ideally, someone on the team is the lead to craft the values, but you can use a third-party consultant, or have a member of the Mars group that is trusted and supported by the whole group craft the statements. The lead, or the entire group, should examine the themes and begin to come up with draft value statements using those themes or words.

If there is one thing to avoid it is getting tangled up with the vanilla statements about integrity, respect, performance, honesty, commitment, sustainability, achievement. These are table stakes. An organization should not have to articulate values such as those—everyone should bring them every day. Don't create values that could be featured on one of those terrible posters of rowing teams, lighthouses and sunsets that adorn many an office wall. That, sadly, represents about 99% of the world's organizational value statements. Don't go there.

Instead, be inspiring and memorable. Create statements that are bold and provocative. Statements that resonate with people and plant a stake in the ground. Statements that really reflect you, and your aspirations for your organization.

Developing these value statements will take time, and your team may have to review a few drafts to get a good solid cut of them. Each member of the team should receive them in advance of a meeting to discuss everyone's views. The CEO should be actively involved but needs to create the space for the whole team to feel like they are actively shaping the values.

Once the team has landed on some dynamic value statements, create a short narrative for each one that tells a story or two about what that value statement means. These narratives should represent what living that value is all about: what someone will be doing if they live up to it; the challenges or decisions they will face when encountered with a values conflict. Give each narrative some life, some personality and some contextual meaning. If possible, identify heroes of the organization that have lived that value particularly well and animate the narrative with their story.

Finally, select 10-12 words that summarize what each value is all about—individual characteristics or expected behaviours associated with each value statement. These are often some of the words that were originally part of the value theme but didn't make the final cut due to brevity and editing. These words should reflect what the value statement means.

Congratulations, you now have your new values.

At the Calgary Chamber, our process yielded four value statements:

1. Make an impact.
2. Do what's right.
3. Never stop pushing.
4. Get it done.

I assure you, every team member can recite them off by heart. These value statements are memorable, compelling, meaningful and energizing.

Activating the Values: Becoming the Culture

Now that the values have been refreshed, it is time to roll them out. Here are some ideas as to how to activate the new values:

- Hold an all-staff meeting to unveil the new values. Ask members of the Mars group to pick one value that means the most to them, create and read to the whole team why it is important to them, and acknowledge another staff member who lives this value using specific examples to bring it to life.

- Create visibility for the new values (large stickers on the wall, screen savers, etc.).

- Give everyone something to remind them of the values every day. At the Calgary Chamber, everyone got a mug that had a value on it.

- Integrate the new values into the hiring process (as discussed in Chapter 8).

- Include living the values as part of performance appraisals.

- Change your employee handbook, orientation material and other key documents to reflect the new values.

- Each week at an all-staff check-in, ask people to mention a "values champion"—someone who did a great job living the values last week—for group recognition and acknowledgement.

- Put the values at the top of board agendas and meeting materials.

- Continually reinforce the values repeatedly at every chance.

Over time, the right people you want on the team will get behind these values. Those who do not may not be the right fit for the organization. Their failure or reluctance to live the values provides rationale for their departure. A strong set of values that reflect the best people is one of the best filters an organization can have for ensuring that all people on the team are the right ones.

If done properly, and at an opportune time, the new values should win over most people. However, some people, including your board, may push back. "Where is respect? Where is integrity?" Don't be surprised. Many people have been indoctrinated to think those should be organizational values. And they are important values—for individuals. But they are not organizational values or team values.

No CEO or set of organizational values should have to remind people that they need to be respectful or hard working in their role. If they aren't, why do they have a job? Be very clear that the absence of important individual values does not mean that you don't value them, it just means that you expect and demand them from everyone so much so that you don't need to put them on the wall.

As people recognize each other for living the values, or as more people are hired that align to the values, and as more people can recite the values by memory, you'll see signs that you've shifted culture. Your culture is the living out and operationalization of your values.

Resource Kit

Ask This—Diagnostic 2

(You can complete all diagnostic questions from each chapter online at www.makingremarkable.com)
Use a rating of Yes=1, No=0. A score of 80% or better indicates that you are likely remarkable in that element.

1. The Values
   a. Do you have organizational values?
   b. Were your organizational values reviewed or refreshed within the last three years?
   c. Are your values inspiring and meaningfully connected to your specific organization and team (i.e., beyond the traditional words such as "respect," "trust," "achieve," etc.)?
   d. Does your organization have a culture that is defined by your established values (i.e., does your culture reflect the values?)
   e. Were your values constructed with the engagement of your top performers and key customers/members and stakeholders?

2. Living the Values
   a. Can at least 80% of the team recite the organizational values from memory?
   b. Are the values visible in the organization (i.e., on the wall, on mugs, on screensavers, on report covers, etc.)?
   c. Are values reinforced during regular activity such as weekly meetings, rewards and recognition programs, and performance reviews?

d. Do you spend time as a team celebrating people who live and embody the values on a regular basis?

e. Do you use the values as part of your hiring process? Specifically, are values interviews conducted to ensure that any new hires reflect the existing values?

Do This to be Remarkable

- Believe in the importance and power of culture.
  - Don't believe that you can achieve remarkable outcomes within an unremarkable culture. If you want to be a remarkable organization, you need a culture that will attract and inspire people to perform in ways that create remarkability.

- Come to the party prepared.
  - As a new CEO or leader, have a sense of the desired values and culture that you want for your organization and team. This will enable you to assess what is there against what you want and to determine a plan.

- Assess what is there.
  - A culture already exists, whether it is the one you want it to be or not. Be prepared to convince people of the need for a changed culture.
  - Observe and examine the activities, behaviours and approaches of the staff you have inherited. Their behaviours will give you insight into the culture that exists, regardless of what may be espoused as the values.

- Build a Mars group to (re)craft your values.
  - Pick who on your team you want to help re-craft the values and bring them together.
  - Don't get sucked into using vanilla and useless words like "trust" and "integrity"—be bold, be inspirational, be authentic.

- Activate the values.
  - Make values a key part of the HR process – hiring, firing, advancement and rewarding
  - Find ways to bring your values to life through visuals, repetition and reinforcement.
  - Embed values into process, procedure and policy, as well as into strategy and resource allocation decisions.
  - Engage staff in recognizing those who are values exemplars.

Review This

- BOOKS
  - Simon Sinek, *Leaders Eat Last: Why Some Teams Pull Together and Others Don't.* Portfolio/Penguin (2014).
  - Paul Marciano, *Carrots and Sticks Don't Work: Build a Culture of Employee Engagement Built on the Principles of RESPECT.* McGraw-Hill Education (2010).
  - Jeremy Gutsche, *Exploiting Chaos: 150 Ways to Spark Innovation During Times of Change.* Gotham Books (2009).
  - Howard Schultz, *Onward: How Starbucks Fought for Its Life without Losing Its Soul.* Rodale (2011).

- ○ Jason Fried and David Heinemeier Hansson, *REWORK*. Crown Business (2010).

- OTHER
  - ○ http://www.jimcollins.com/article_topics/articles/aligning-action.html
  - ○ https://cultureiq.com/5-ted-talks-inspire-great-company-culture/

PEOPLE

While Purpose is the bedrock of any organization and the starting point for its transformational journey to remarkability, People are the most important ingredient in a thriving organization.

The People pillar of remarkability is comprised of two elements:

1. Your Board of Directors
2. A Remarkable Team

Let's look at each one in turn.

CHAPTER 7: People: Your Board of Directors

What is it?	Your board is the body that governs the organization, oversees your work and performance, and will provide you with support and approvals for change and transformation. Their role is to ensure that the organization performs today, and to oversee the sustainability and future success of the organization.
Why is it important?	A high-performing, trusting board can make the job of a CEO much easier, so you can focus your time and energy on real outcomes and change.
Where do you start?	• Understand the state of the board through interviews and/or surveys. • Assess the board you are working with. • Identify where the board needs improvement or if there is a need to improve your relationship with, and trust level from, the board.

Remarkable is:	• A highly trusting and respectful relationship between board and executive
	• A regular practice of board engagement
	• A high-performing board that has the right:
	   o Focus: on the future, long-term outcomes, strategy, governance and fiduciary responsibility
	   o Form: of diverse and skilled director composition, essential committee structure
	   o Frame: of effective and efficient governing policies and procedures, and streamlined meeting format

"Good governance…is essential to an organization's long-term success." Mac Van Wielingen[11]

The board is your boss. They decide your fate and your future. They will be your greatest cheerleader—and will also be judge and jury of the work that you do as the head of your organization. It's vital that you establish a collaborative and trusting relationship between CEO and board so that they can give you, the CEO, permission to undertake organizational transformation into remarkability.

Ideally, you have come on board in a spirit of renewal and excitement, and you have been hired to make changes. In such a scenario, the board is typically onside with a Remarkability Agenda; their support generates the ability to make changes and take (sometimes uncomfortable) risks. However, in some instances, the board will not be behind you and you will need to work to establish trust and approval for your Agenda. Both these instances will be explored throughout this chapter.

Governance isn't a sexy topic, but it's important in terms of the CEO's ability to effect change, get the needed resources and implement an Agenda. It is also about where the board focuses its attention. The motivations of board members and the effectiveness of its time spent together will play a significant role in how much time the CEO needs to spend on managing the board versus executing the plan and will also serve to play a meaningful role in the direction, activities and success of the organization.

This chapter is about a high-performing board and how to devise a modern approach to governance that will help you work together to achieve remarkability. Having the right people on your board is very important—but having them act in ways that optimize their governance function is just as much so.

The Relationship Dynamic: Trust

The relationship dynamic between a board and its leader is about one thing: trust. If they have trust in you, the board will support you as you work to transform the organization.

Trust, however, is not infinite—it is like a reservoir—and once established, it must be regularly renewed and replenished. By ensuring that the reservoir of trust and faith remains high, the CEO has the support to implement the Remarkability Agenda, ask for resources, and avoid being micro-managed. Trust will ensure that the board remains hands-off and focuses on the strategic and governance level.

So, how do you build trust? Besides some of the table stakes—like honesty, integrity, ethics and respect—trust is built daily through action and performance. Specifically, building and replenishing the trust reservoir requires:

- Demonstrable progress in your role generally, and those initiatives or actions deemed critical by the board
- Proof points of success, traction or change
- Improvement in the measures of success

Generally speaking, you have been hired as a change agent and the reservoir of trust should be full at the outset of your tenure. Having just completed the search and hiring process, the board should have optimism and faith in you. Use that trust early on to ask probing or difficult questions that will get to the core of any board-related issues and to test transformation ideas as they emerge from your work. These early discussions will let you know if you have a substantial reservoir of trust and if the board will support your ideas for transformation.

However, if you feel that your reservoir of trust is low amongst the board, or even segments of the board, tackle the issue head on by working to understand what lies at the root of this low level of trust and then move to address the situation. Avoiding or ignoring a low level of trust rarely results in longevity for a leader. To be successful and, frankly, to remain in the role, you need the trust of your board.

A CEO should never take the trust reservoir for granted. They should always focus on execution and performance to ensure that the trust reservoir remains full, because that's what will enable them to get things done.

Get to Know Your Board

It's a fact: the board decides your evaluations, pay, bonus, time off, and how enjoyable or painful your working life will be. It is simply common sense to establish a good working relationship with as many of your board members as possible.

Get to know them: the roles that they play within their organizations, how they want to contribute on your board, and what their motivations are for being on the board in the first place. Do they believe in the purpose of the organization, or are they there to add something to their resume, grow their profile or advance a pet project? Knowing who they are and what motivates them can make your job easier and help you find ways to make their time spent on the board more rewarding— something they will appreciate.

I made it a priority to build strong relationships with each of my board members, and to maintain open channels of communication with every one of them. I met individually with each one at least once a year for a meal or informal catch up to understand how they felt I was performing, how the team was doing, and how we were executing against our plan and budget. I would also learn whether they enjoyed serving on the board, and if they had any specific ideas or ways in which they wanted to contribute. This was often a chance to discuss any sensitive issues, or any issues that they were uncomfortable raising in the bigger forum.

Even more important is ensuring a strong and trusting relationship with your board chair. I held minimum monthly meetings with my board chairs to go over the strategic, governance and operational matters I wanted them to understand, and those items where I needed their support and approval. I also aimed to have a meal with my chair a couple of times a year to establish a close and trusting relationship. Hosting a dinner with your spouse/partner and the board chair and their spouse/partner can also serve as a means of recognizing and appreciating the extra work that they do, and the support of their spouse in doing so.

Treating the board well is critical. You must recognize that they are all volunteers and doing this in addition to their paid roles. At the Calgary Chamber, our board has free access to all our events, gets special invites to exclusive functions, an annual dinner and other small things that let them know that we as staff value the time and contributions they make each year. That investment will pay dividends for your success in the role.

Evolving Board Governance

In *Race for Relevance,* Coerver and Byers outline five key changes needed for associations to recapture their relevance and impact in today's changing society. Of those five changes, three of them are related to board and governance:

1. Overhaul the governance model: reduce the size of the board and make sure that it is focused at the strategy and governance level.
2. Overhaul committees: eliminate the executive committee and task other committees with being focused and outcome oriented.
3. Empower the CEO and enhance staff: give the CEO more authority and accountability and enhance the role of staff to be more effective.

Having implemented these changes at the Calgary Chamber, I completely agree that they are critical to creating a high-performing board. While I was fortunate to have an incredible board that had a high degree of trust in me, I had to earn it and, working with multiple board chairs, make some changes that would enable the board to become high-performing. Neither my Remarkability Agenda, nor the remarkable organization we became, could have been achieved with a low-performing board, and it is unlikely yours will either.

When I arrived at the Calgary Chamber, the board was comprised of great people, but it had its challenges. Too much time was spent looking backwards and at operations, and very little on strategy. The board was keen to get into the details of our next event which hindered our ability to build a solid plan for the future. While the financial results warranted some deeper dives, we did dive too deep.

I recognized that we needed to improve the focus and approach of our board. I proposed the concept of bringing Harrison Coerver in for a board session on adopting the principles espoused in *Race for Relevance* to my board chair. I convinced him to do so by saying that for us to regain our relevance and our impact in the community, we needed to transform our governance and our board. Efforts to change brand and models would only go so far if we didn't have the right governance and a high-performing board.

This was a difficult conversation because it required me to identify the areas where the board was not performing. While I admired and appreciated every single member of that early board, we needed them to perform at a higher level.

My board chair agreed and approved hiring Coerver to come and facilitate a session. Coerver took us through some of the key principles on governance, specifically the size of the board, the focus of the board, committee structures and composition. It was an incredibly productive session but an incredibly tense one, too. It was a session that got to the core of our why and our goals, and there were many disagreements that occurred over the size, focus and level of engagement.

Some board members didn't want to go too small. Others did. Some board members wanted to keep their fingers on the operational details, while others didn't. Some board members knew we needed some more senior executives on our board, while others felt they fit the bill as the right people.

In the end, most of the board got to a place where we would almost halve the board over two years from 20 people to 12, would eliminate the Executive Committee, and would focus only on strategy and governance, leaving operational details to staff overseen by the board standing committees.

This took courage, commitment, and selflessness. I have an immense amount of respect, gratitude and admiration for those 20 people, for they have helped play a key role in the Calgary Chamber's transformation.

The High Performing Board: The Three Fs

To deliver a Remarkability Agenda, you will need a high-performing board. A high-performing board is about three Fs: it must have the right:

1. Focus: on the future, long-term outcomes, strategy, governance and fiduciary responsibility
2. Form: of people and skills based on needs and culture, diversity, size and terms, and committee structure
3. Frame: of effective and efficient governing policies and procedures, and streamlined meeting agendas

A high-performing board is one that oversees the performance of today to ensure that the organization is on track to be doing even better tomorrow. They need to be keeping an eye on today, while focused on the long-term future of the organization.

A high-performing board is one that supports, enables and empowers you, and helps to provide guidance and clarity for the future. It is one that knows its focus, is set up in terms of the right form to keep that focus and has a frame in place that will enable it to be a forward-looking, high-performing board. In short, it is a modern approach to governance that enables remarkability.

Focus

A high-performing board needs to have the right focus, and that should be forward-looking and oriented towards the future. The board should be looking to future opportunities and risks in the changing world around us because they cannot affect the outcome of things that have already happened, only the things that are going to happen. A poorly executed event, for example, is in the past; other than understanding what went wrong, a board's time is not well spent looking back. Leave that work to the committees and management.

The right level of focus for a high-performing board operating with more modern governance is to be looking at, discussing and considering things at the strategic level, focused on the key financial and fiduciary matters, risk management, health of and adherence to corporate culture, discussion and identification of future opportunities and growth, and the issues of change affecting the organization. The board should be asking about trends, opportunities, economic conditions, key issues of customers/membership or bringing in guest speakers. Barring any serious concern over staff performance, operational issues or management responsibilities are outside the focus of good board governance.

The old model of boards digging into operations, being the spokespeople, bringing in pet projects, and taking authority more appropriate for staff is outdated. These kinds of boards were set up in an era when serving on a board was about heavy work commitment or meant to provide people with purpose and comradeship. Those days are over. Organizations cannot flourish with that kind of board engagement and approach. If this is your situation, this chapter will speak to options and ideas.

When I arrived at the Calgary Chamber, most board and committee time was spent looking backwards, analyzing why performance was what it was (generally poor), and justifying past actions and decisions. It hindered our ability to dig deeper and address the challenges facing us now and, in the future, and to tap into the expertise and guidance of the board as to what might work to improve results going forward.

It was around the time that our organizational performance improved that our board meetings at the Calgary Chamber improved. As we redefined our brand, purpose, value proposition and as new board members joined, the team produced better results, therefore we were able to start looking forward. It got to a point where our board indicated that we could stop looking back so much and instead build a board agenda and program around the future. It was an interesting place to be, having built a reflex for board meetings that were all about the past and justifying past actions and performance. We had to un-learn that muscle memory and instead build new responses to adjust to a future-first orientation. It took time, and guidance from our top board members and chairs, but we got there. We got to a place that made our meetings and agendas far more efficient and effective.

At the Calgary Chamber, the committees assess historical performance and then determine if there are any major issues to be addressed at the board level. The board, staff and committees provide written reports about past performance and lessons learned including any actions or remedies to be taken. This all becomes part of the consent agenda and is assumed to have been read, including commitment of the committees and board to monitor any actions that need to be taken to address performance related issues. The focus of board meetings is discussing the upcoming quarters, and what is being done to ensure that targets are met, past lessons learned, risks, opportunities, or to discuss strategic issues like digital investments.

One of the best means of ensuring good focus for a board is to recruit strong senior people who will self-police their colleagues. Senior and busy business leaders have no interest in participating in discussions that look back too much, dig into the details or get lost in the weeds. They'll call each other out if they're headed into unproductive territory and will get any discussion or focus back on track.

Boards need to also focus on the long-term performance of the organization. The trap of short-termism is all too common these days, with both for- and non-profit organizational leadership making choices that may create positive outcomes in the short-term, but don't generate as strong a long-term outcome, or in a worst-case scenario can have a negative impact on the long-term achievement of an organization's purpose and key results. Therefore, boards should regularly require that management provide proof of progress towards an organizational purpose and the long-term objectives. This may be through an annual presentation of performance metrics or a review of progress towards strategic plan targets. Regardless of how it is done, a board must keep its focus long-term and ensure leadership is demonstrating progress towards that.

An excellent way to keep discussions focused on the future is to deliver meaningful work and seek the board's input on pre-prepared questions. At the Calgary Chamber, each year I delivered a State of the Chamber presentation to the board. It lasted about an hour and covered topics such as summary of key performance metrics, comparison of our chamber to our peers using ACCE Dynamic Chamber Benchmarking, trends happening in the world around us (economic, social, technological), staff survey results, member survey results and ideas for the future.

I would send 2-3 big questions for the board to consider in advance of our meeting; we then held a discussion on those questions after the presentation. By doing this we got great generative discussion from them, and a lot of insight and value. Delivering this kind of work and analysis is a critical part of any CEO's role and will keep the board focused at the right level.

Questions you should consider in terms of your board's focus include:

1. How would you describe the board's focus: is it backward-looking, forward-looking, strategic, or operational?

2. Does the board spend enough time understanding the future, risks to the organization, and opportunities to be explored?

3. Does the board regularly hold leadership accountable for progress towards the organizational purpose and long-term targets?

4. What do you see as the division between board and CEO roles? (Note that this can be particularly important as many boards see the chair as the lead spokesperson for the organization. Understanding expectations and boundaries early on is important.)

5. Is the board effective, in your opinion? What could be improved?

6. Does the board, as a whole or individually, stay at the right governance, strategic and fiduciary level in its deliberations, thoughts and actions, or does it get into management or operational issues?

In summary, the right focus for a high-performing board is:
- The future—forward looking
- The long term
- Strategy
- Performance

- Fiduciary and oversight matters
- Risk, opportunity and change affecting the organization
- Culture
- How to support the CEO and staff in achieving performance

Form

You need the right people on the board at the right time, for the right reasons. A remarkable organization's board form is about three things:

1. The right people and skills
2. The right size and terms
3. The right committees

People and Skills

The right people and skills will make or break the effectiveness of the board, and ultimately the organization. With the right thoughtful, engaged, future-focused and experienced people, the CEO's job is easy and effective. But have the wrong people who are there for the wrong reason and lack the needed skills and competencies, and the CEO's job is a living nightmare and the organization is ineffective.

High-performing boards have members that are there for the right reason; they believe in the purpose of the organization and want to help ensure it succeeds over the long-term. They are not there to pad a resume or gain some board experience. For a high-performing board and a remarkable organization, you need people who believe in the purpose, are there to help, have no agenda, and don't need this on their resume.

Your board will need directors who have the right experience—in governance, leadership and strategy—so they can contribute meaningfully to your Remarkability Agenda and to your organization's strategic targets. There should be a bar to pass to be considered an effective and desirable board member. Without previous governance experience, people will be dragging you into the weeds. Without leadership experience, they won't be able to help you make leader-oriented decisions. And finally, if they don't have strategy experience, they will have a hard time being future-focused and strategy-oriented. These must be required bases of experience that each board member has to keep board efforts at the right level.

A board should identify the skills and competencies that directors <u>must</u> have to be strong contributors to the board and provide strategic counsel to the CEO and management, as well as those that are <u>desired</u> based on what is needed in the current strategy. Required skills are those that are table stakes and are essential to being considered for the board. The desired skills are those that are an ideal fit for the organization based on where it is at in terms of its strategy and the opportunities and challenges that it currently faces. Create a matrix that maps current directors against required and desired skill sets, to identify gaps and identify succession requirements. The desired skills and competencies that have gaps and succession potential should be the ones used to recruit and filter people in or out of potential for a seat on the board.

For example, in 2016, the Calgary Chamber board wanted to expand its knowledge in the digital and technology arena. That was a part of our new strategy and was clearly a gap on the board from a strategic standpoint. Therefore, the board worked to promote the need for digital and technology skills and then recruit someone of that background.

Once a board has defined its focus, as discussed in the section above, that focus and approach to how they govern is a large part of the board culture. While they have fiduciary, governing and even (depending on the organization) legislative responsibilities, the values and behaviours of directors, and the way in which the individuals interact, work together, address issues, assess organizational performance and focus their energies and efforts is the board culture. Mac Van Wielingen argues convincingly for robust board cultures in his report *The Evolving Role of the Corporate Board Part 2: Culture as Governance and the Link with Performance* published by his Viewpoint Group[12]. Ensuring that a high-performing board stays high-performing is about creating collaborations, structures and process that enable current and future board members to continue the high-performance form and focus. These mechanisms and processes should be included in board recruitment, succession and orientation efforts. Boards may find it advantageous to articulate and define their board culture (e.g., what they value, how they assess performance, what is important and how they operate etc.), if for no other reason than to support recruitment activities.

To ensure that your board gets the right people in terms of experience, skills and competencies, create board member job descriptions that explicitly state the required and desired skills and competencies (i.e., leadership, governance, financial literacy, etc.) that are table stakes for being considered. Board job descriptions should also articulate the board culture so that there is less risk of a poor fit and bringing on people who won't keep the right focus. These descriptions should include expectations of directors in terms of focus, performance, duty, responsibility and participation. Board recruitment information or material should clearly define the culture, desired skills and competencies that align to the strategic needs of the board at any given time and be clear about who you are seeking.

Diversity on boards is another key compositional consideration. Gender, ethnicity, and age are just a few diversity lenses through which to look at your board composition. But there are other lenses of diversity that will add to the richness of your board and its work. Board members who can bring different and fresh perspectives to strategy and opportunities are extremely valuable for navigating the future.

For example, how many boards have a millennial who can provide insight into their generation, or a digital expert who can speak to technological trends? How many boards have adequate female representation to address equity concerns? How many boards have LGBTQ representation to ensure that inclusiveness is fostered as part of the DNA and purpose of the organization? These and other kinds of diverse perspectives add significant value in bringing a different view and voice to the table.

To ensure you get the right people and skills, the CEO should work with an appropriate board committee (e.g., nominating or governance and HR committee) to create a process that puts these pieces together clearly, transparently and openly for all to see and understand. It can then be used by board members to recruit and filter for the right board candidates. A high-performing board has a well-documented recruitment, selection and evaluation process that creates a consistent and repeatable framework that will deliver the right people to serve on your board.

While aiming to fill the board with strategic skill sets and expertise, boards should never be oriented towards composition based on representations of constituencies or filling seats based on connection in the community. Many associations and chambers fall into the trap of bringing on someone because they represent some geographic, organizational or demographic domain. Avoid this. You lose control of the quality of people you bring onto the board and are forced into a box-checking exercise rather than being purposeful about achieving a high-performing board.

The final step is orientation. All high-performing boards have a comprehensive onboarding and orientation process that enables board members to hit their stride as soon as possible. Having a clear set of documentation to provide, as well as coaching and support from experienced board members, can orient new members quickly and effectively.

In the end, a high-performing board will work hard to ensure it has, and continues to have, the right people. It will have clearly identified required and desired skills, competencies and experience, an articulated culture, and a means of identifying who is needed at certain times based on a succession plan. An interviewing and evaluating process should be developed so that candidates can be assessed for their match and fit. Recruitment and nomination efforts should adhere to these requirements. Following these guidelines will enable you to ensure that future boards are set up to attract and retain the right people.

Size and Terms

While rarely an issue in Canada, the size of boards can also be an issue. Some boards of organizations like chambers of commerce in the U.S. are upwards of 50-70 people. This is way too large. At the Calgary Chamber, we found a board of 12-14 to work well. Bigger isn't always better, so find the right size that works for your organization.

Boards that have between 10-14 people often have enough people to create diversity of experience and perspectives and can allocate enough people to committees. I have found that to be an ideal size range.

Of course, a board is not always about size but about commitment and engagement. During recruitment, make clear that there is an expectation of regular attendance and engagement in the discussions, work and decisions.

Term limits for board members are also important to encourage fresh ideas and energy. A preferred structure is typically two terms of three years each to enable a board member to learn the business and be able to contribute. Staggered terms help ensure that there is regular turnover of people without losing so many in any given year that it would put governance or stability at risk. You will still have enough people who can remember some recent history.

Committees

High-performing boards also put a lot of time, thought and consideration into their committees and committee structure. Using committee structures appropriately is also a way to ensure that the focus at the board level remains in the right place. A fundamental aspect of high-performing boards is to keep the number of committees small and focused only on those areas in which the board needs to be involved.

The board needs to purposefully stay involved in key governance, fiduciary and strategy areas, and purposefully stay out of operational areas. Governance, HR, finance, audit and risk, innovation, and investments are all acceptable and desirable focus areas for committees because they are about oversight, the future and strategy. But fundraising, events, programs, membership, and marketing are all areas that the board should not be engaged in from a committee perspective as they are too operational. If they do want to get into the operational matters they need to volunteer in that capacity, and they should do so clearly and distinctly as a volunteer to not confuse the two roles for themselves or for staff.

Committees are where the "work" and the historical review will happen. That makes sense as they are more working-group-oriented than the full governance function of the board.

Many boards are eliminating the executive committee to ensure that there is good engagement from the whole board; often, the executive committee is making all the decisions with the full board merely rubber stamping. This doesn't take advantage of the diversity of skills and perspectives that each board member can bring to the table and can create disengaged directors.

Questions you should consider in terms of your board's form include:

1. Is the board comprised of people who are there for the right reasons?

2. Do the people on the board have the right experience, skill sets and competencies to be high-performing? What might be missing? What do you no longer need?

3. Is the board sufficiently diverse?

4. Are new board members oriented adequately?

5. Do you have good articulation of board culture and director job descriptions?

6. Are board terms and succession adequate? Do you have the right means of recruiting the best candidates?

7. Is the board the right size?

8. Do you feel that you have the right committees? If not, what should you add? What should you drop?

9. Are the committees being effective? Are committee mandates focused on the right things? Are committees producing what they should be?

In summary, the right form for a high-performing board is:

- The right people there for the right reasons, at the right time, with the right experience, skills and competencies matched to the strategic needs of the organization
- Diverse
- Well-defined in terms of culture and role
- Well recruited and vetted
- Oriented to their role
- Fostered through rigour in the recruitment and orientation process using thorough skills matrix, job descriptions and orientation processes and tools
- The right size of board and committees, and right length of term
- The right number, and focus, of committees on issues of governance, strategy and fiduciary responsibility
- Comprised of effective committees that do essential work for the board, and do not excessively burden staff

Frame

The frame of a high-performing board includes bylaws, policies, procedures, terms of reference, and board meeting structures and agendas. A CEO should seek to close any gaps in these frames, but also look for excessive structure and opportunities to cut and streamline. Excessive burden in terms of bylaws, reporting and analysis for the sake of policies, and procedures that restrict the ability of leaders to make good decisions and use appropriate judgement are all detrimental to a remarkable organizational model needed for today.

High-performing boards need good and effective policies and procedures. They should be reviewed regularly and kept up to date, streamlined for any unnecessary or outdated information. They should cover areas like authorities, roles, accountabilities, behaviours, focus, meeting and agenda approaches etc. Policies should cover areas such as conflicts, code of conduct, fitness to serve, confidentiality, liability and others. Often, the board and its committees should have these baked into policy, procedure and terms of reference. These all exist to provide the frame to enable a board to meaningfully, safely and effectively exercise their fiduciary and governance responsibilities.

One of my best board members at the Chamber, an executive vice president of a major publicly-traded Canadian company, always kept us focused on having that right balance of policy and procedure that enabled us to do our work but didn't bog us down in analysis, reporting and needless work. For example, at one meeting of the Governance and HR Committee, management was tasked with reviewing the terms of reference and reporting back on our alignment. We determined that we were not fully in compliance with a policy that stated that the committee must assess management's adherence to operational policy.

We could have tackled this problem in many ways, ranging from the excessively complex and onerous to the simple and basic. This board member indicated that at his company there was a whole department established to evaluate and demonstrate adherence to policy. He suggested that measures requiring management to produce excessive reports and spend time on this exercise was just that—excessive. Instead, he proposed a declaration produced by the CEO that would have several representative checks and balances for key policy items. As a result, a potentially time-consuming and onerous task that didn't drive value to members was averted and we kept it simple yet effective and compliant. I can't thank him enough

There is a calibration of policy and procedure that creates the right balance between responsibility and flexibility. Working with experienced leaders on your board or committees can help to find that right calibration, implement it, and adjust as necessary. Policy and procedure are there to guide, enable and protect leaders, not needlessly curtail, restrain or burden them. Therefore, pare down work that analyzes the past and bogs management down in reporting and unnecessary analysis. Frames should exist to support the execution of objectives, and the achievement of opportunity through creating enhanced value for the customer or member. All bylaws, policy, procedures and committee terms of reference should be reviewed regularly—every two to three years to ensure they reflect this spirit and nature.

Board meeting formats and agendas can also help your board become and stay high- performing. Many organizations run into the trap of feeling they must meet frequently—as in monthly to exercise their duties. That is fallacy. Your board should be meeting between four and six times a year, maximum, enabling the staff to focus on executing plans. Committees should be where the work happens from a board perspective, and they too should meet about four to six times a year.

High-performing board meeting agendas should be crafted such that most items, particularly those addressed by committees or are backward looking, are in the consent agenda. Putting as much content as possible into consent agendas (including committee reports and minutes, operational updates and other basic content) is one way to reduce the often limited-value discussions that can take place on minute details. Directors are assumed to have read it, and by adopting the consent agenda in the meeting, they are declaring they are informed and supportive of its contents.

The bulk of the agenda should be oriented towards decision making and strategic discussion on items such as:

- Next quarter's plan: definitions of success and how to achieve it
- Key risks the organization is facing right now
- Trends and foresight, new opportunities
- Presentation and discussions on market research with members, customers and the community
- Reviewing project/concept proposals or research from staff that create new opportunities or value for customers/members
- Guest speakers such as customers, members or an expert in a certain field of interest or relevance to the organization

Questions you should consider in terms of your board's frame include:

1. Do you feel that the board needs any changes to policies or process?

2. Are there any policy gaps?

3. Are any policies creating unnecessary process or work?

4. Do all committees have adequate and clear terms of reference?

5. Are you satisfied with the format and time allocations spent at board meetings and committee meetings (time, duration, focus, etc.)?

In summary, the right frame for a high-performing board is:

- Modern policies and procedures
- Processes and oversight that do not excessively burden staff with reporting
- Current and clear terms of reference
- A regular review cycle for all board governance documents that does not extend past three years
- The right number of meetings, with the right focus and agendas

Board Support for Becoming High-Performing

The reality is that most boards need some work to become truly high- performing, and you will probably need to spend some time improving the board's focus, form or frame. Working with the board on such changes can be sensitive because it amounts to self-diagnosis, much honesty and self-reflection, and potentially an admission of underperformance.

To generate endorsement for board development work, you will need the support of an executive-level champion, or someone whom you trust and is also influential on the board. This may be a chair, vice chair, or someone who has the gravitas or trust on the board. To build the case, you should communicate areas of potential improvement that will bring the organizational performance to a new level by getting them aligned to the right focus, form or frame. This includes some of the rationale discussed in the previous section, appealing to their notion of legacy, and supporting your ability to make an effective and impactful transformation to become remarkable.

The ability to work with your chair or your board to bring about improvement and movement toward higher performance will not be a slam-dunk for everyone. If you're successful in garnering support, the section below will outline a process. If you're not successful, or don't think the timing is right, the section at the end of the chapter will outline some strategies to get there.

Once you have your champion or support, it is time to better understand the state of the board so that you can address the areas of shortfall and build a plan for improvement.

Understanding Board Performance and Creating a Plan

You will want to get an assessment of the state of each of the three Fs of a high-performing board, and then develop your plan using the results of that assessment in collaboration with your board champion or designated committee. To do this, you should hold one-on-one interviews with the board individually, or through a survey, third-party advisor, or focus group. These should focus on focus, form and frame using the questions just provided earlier in this chapter. The key is to be able to gather the insights of the board in a way that creates opportunity for improvement.

Another option to consider is to conduct a confidential board assessment survey. Here, the board members rate and score their own performance as a board and have the chance to anonymously raise concerns or issues. Some of these surveys also ask directors to rate and evaluate the performance of their fellow directors. These are often completed by an independent third party. They can be helpful and insightful as a measure to track performance and improvement over time.

Unless the board is a high-performing board comprised of senior people who are strong in leadership and governance, the discussions, interviews and board assessment surveys will often reveal concerns about being too stuck in the weeds, some elements of dysfunction and beliefs that some people either aren't pulling their weight or that they are wasting time on issues that are not important to the board or at the right level for the board to be addressing. This is to be expected. Few boards are perfect and there will always be ways in which a board can improve. So, don't be surprised or put off by the results. Use them as good data and insight into where to focus to get the board performing at a higher level.

Summarizing all the information and insight you have on the board, including your original assessment (from Chapter 4), the one-on-one interviews, and the board assessment survey results if undertaken, into a consolidated report will help to identify the elements of focus, form and frame that need to be addressed. Working with the committee or task force and holding a board strategic discussion will be valuable to help gain agreement on the key issues and strategic priorities and may in fact set the course for significant change and improvement. This session should be done as a special event or one-off session. It should be done with a third-party facilitator to ensure that neither the CEO nor the board's agenda is the focal point, and that there is sound collaboration working through the issues. You will then take what you have learned from this board engagement and create a plan that will transition the board into one that is more high-performing.

A Low-Performing Board: What to do About It

You may be reading this and saying to yourself "this is all lovely, but it's wishful thinking for me. I don't have a high-performing board. And I don't think I can get it to be one either. They won't go for this."

I hear you. This stuff isn't easy.

There are many reasons why the board, or individual board members, may resist change:

1. Recognition that they are not the kind of person who could serve on a high-performing board but fear of acknowledging that

2. Reluctance to give up the status or profile that comes with serving on a very active or high-profile board

3. Loss of a purpose or sense of meaning

4. Loss of friends or comradeship

5. Loss of opportunity to address their personal issue or agenda

6. Resistance to change generally, or a belief that the change isn't needed

Regardless of the rationale for why they would not want to become high-performing, you will need to evaluate the situation and decide possible paths to take. Ask yourself:

- Is this a short-term thing that you can ride out?

- Is another board chair coming who will support your Remarkability Agenda and drive for transformation and improvement—particularly at the board level?

- Are there any data points, examples, case studies, or speakers that you can bring in to demonstrate or articulate the imperative to become a high-performing board?

- Can you bring the person/people on side?

- Are there points of alignment or commonality that you can use as footholds of agreement for the larger change?

- Are they actively undermining you or looking to have you replaced? Do you have more allies than enemies?

- Do you have the confidence of the chair and the subsequent chairs?

Ultimately, you will have to assess whether work to improve the board or its function is possible, and if so, when. There are a few options to consider, depending upon your read of the situation:

1. Continue over time to advocate for board improvement, with an emphasis on convincing other people to support the concept or generate further evidence that will help to bolster your case.

2. Wait for a different chair, leadership or board composition that might be more open to growth and improvement.

3. Drop the case altogether.

It's worth spending time assessing the situation and then seeking guidance from peers, mentors, advisors, and others in a trusted position. Their insights will enable you to develop the best plan for your situation. Regardless of the rationale for any resistance to becoming a high-performing board, or to your Agenda, it is always worth the effort to try and bring people on side and make progress if possible.

Perhaps some of the following approaches might help you convince people to support board change:

- Appeal to their notion of legacy. Let them know that if they support and participate in a broader board change leading to an organizational transformation, they will be remembered as being part of that courageous and thoughtful board that worked to leave a legacy of a better organization.

- Work with data as much as you can to paint the picture of the need for change, the areas of improvement needed and where the organization is struggling because of status quo.

- Bring in outside opinions—sometimes a board will listen more to the opinion of an outsider than they will to their own hired leader. Find a subject matter expert or thought leader that can speak to some of the newer and more modern governance approaches, or someone in the community that supports you and your Remarkability Agenda ideas, and have them speak the board, or to key individuals on the board, in support of the case for improvement.

Regardless of your path, take care to protect yourself mentally, emotionally, and career-wise from any challenging relationships with your board or individuals on it. Assess the situation and decide: is there a chance I can still be successful in this role or is the situation one in which I cannot be successful?

If you think that you can still be successful, keep reading because there is lots more on the Agenda to make your organization remarkable.

If you don't think you can be successful, you may wish to consider a role change, or drop the concept of a transformation. While persistence is a key trait of leaders, persistence with no chance of success and a damaged reputation is not worth it.

Resource Kit

Ask This—Diagnostic 3

(You can complete all diagnostic questions from each chapter online at www.makingremarkable.com)
Use a rating of Yes=1, No=0. A score of 80% or better indicates that you are likely remarkable in that element.

1. Relationship Dynamic
    a. Do you have a trust-based relationship with your board?
    b. Is there a high degree of trust between you and your board?
    c. Do at least 80% of your board members support you (i.e., approving of your performance, support your requests and not actively obstruct or undermine your efforts)?
    d. Are you finding ways to get to know your board members?
    e. Are you meeting regularly with your board members, and specifically your board chair, at least monthly?

2. Board Focus
    a. Does your board focus on the future in its meetings, discussion and analyses and not worry excessively about past events?
    b. Is your board focused on the strategy of the organization, and not on granular operational matters?
    c. Does your board think of impact and performance over the long-term time, versus month to month or quarter by quarter?

    d. Does the board focus on governance matters for which they are responsible, and not delve into matters that are interfering with management and operations?

    e. Does the board focus on its fiduciary responsibility with respect to the financials and operations of the organization but remain at the right depth of their oversight?

3. Board Form

    a. Is the board diverse in composition – age, gender, ethnicity, industry, experience?

    b. Is the board largely comprised of people with governance, strategy and leadership experience?

    c. Does the board plan for future high performing members by articulating the board culture, and developing required and desired skills and competencies for recruitment and evaluation?

    d. Do the board's committees focus appropriately on areas such as governance and HR, finance and audit, and risk?

    e. Is there a defined and effective orientation provided for new board members?

4. Board Frame

    a. Does the board have appropriate policies and procedures in place to support their governance and fiduciary responsibilities?

    b. Are the board policies and procedures easy and efficient to comply with and report on? Do they avoid creating unnecessary and excessively burdensome work for management?

    c. Are board policies, procedures and terms of reference on a regular cycle of review and update (i.e., reviewed, updated and brought forward for re-approval every 2-3 years)?

d. Does the board and its committees hold the right number of meetings (i.e., maximum 6) per year?

e. Does the board and its committees build agendas oriented to discussion on strategy, the future, performance and risk?

Do This to be Remarkable

- Get to know your board and treat them well.
  - ○ Spending time getting to know your board will help to build trust and support and enable you to make their experience more enjoyable.
  - ○ Using interviews or surveys, assess the nature of the board and its individuals to determine whether it is high-performing or needs improvement, and in what areas.

- Actively replenish your trust reservoir.
  - ○ You can't get anything done without trust. Excel in your role, deliver, and keep your trust reservoir high.

- Keep your board high-performing.
  - ○ By maintaining the right focus, form and frame your board will operate at the right level, freeing you up to do your job and make your organization remarkable.
    - ■ Focus: on the future, long-term outcomes, strategy, governance, performance and fiduciary responsibility
    - ■ Form: of people and skills based on needs and culture, diversity, size and terms, and committee structure

- ■ Frame: of effective and efficient governing policies and procedures, and streamlined meeting agendas
- ○ Make sure you create processes and systems that enable you to have the right people, at the right time, for the right reasons on your board. Build recruitment and succession matrices and documentation that will ensure your board has the best people.

Review This

- BOOKS
  - ○ Harrison Coerver and Mary Byers, CAE, *Race for Relevance: 5 Radical Changes for Associations.* ASAE The Centre for Association Leadership (2011).
  - ○ Richard Parsons and Mark Feigen *The Boardroom's Quiet Revolution,* March 2014 Harvard Business Review

- OTHER
  - ○ Mac Van Wielingen "The Evolving Role of the Corporate Board Part 1: Governance, Strategy and the Imperative of Performance" http://www.viewpointgroup.ca/public/images/ Part 1 - Governance Strategy and the Imperative of Performance.pdf
  - ○ Mac Van Wiclingen "The Evolving Role of the Corporate Board Part 2: Culture as Governance and the Link with Performance "http://www.viewpointgroup.ca/public/images/ Part 2 - Culture as Governance and the Link with

Performance - Mac Van Wielingen - 2017 (002).pdf

o National Association of Corporate Directors "Culture as a Corporate Asset" https://www.nacdonline.org/files/NACD%20BRC%20Culture%20as%20Corporate%20Asset.pdf

o Institute of Corporate Directors website and materials - https://www.icd.ca/Resource-Centre.aspx

o National Association of Corporate Directors website and materials: www.nacdonline.org

o Chartered Professional Accountants reports on boards and governance https://www.cpacanada.ca/en/business-and-accounting-resources/strategy-risk-and-governance or www.aicpa.org

o American Society of Association Executives board and governance materials: www.asaecenter.org

o Canadian Society of Association Executives board and governance materials: www.csae.com

CHAPTER 8: People: A Remarkable Team

What is it?	Your people are your staff, colleagues and potentially your volunteers. They are the ones who will work with you to bring your brand and purpose to life and help execute on the strategy and plans.
Why is it important?	Your people, and their fit, skill and drive, will ultimately determine the success of your organization. While every business needs customers, there can be no business without people. People are the engine and lifeblood of your Remarkability Agenda, and critical to success. You must find, and work hard to keep, the right ones.
Where do you start?	<ul><li>Assess the existing organizational structure.</li><li>Assess the team you have.</li><li>Determine/establish your leadership operating system.</li><li>Determine what you need on your leadership team.</li></ul>
Remarkable is:	<ul><li>A high-performing and strong leadership team that has a structured leadership operating system that supports trust, accountability and a team spirit</li><li>A values-based, rigorous approach to HR and hiring people</li><li>A deeply ingrained coaching- and performance-based culture</li><li>Regular means of rewarding, recognizing and surveying team members, tied to your values</li><li>An organization with high team engagement, satisfaction and understanding of what is expected of them</li><li>Treating people well, aligned to values and given meaningful work and opportunities to grow</li></ul>

"The ability of a group of people to do remarkable things hinges on how well those people can pull together as a team."
Simon Sinek[13]

After establishing your purpose, the second most critical part of any successful organization and its remarkability is having the right team. To be successful, an organization needs to have the right people in the right roles, living the values, and aligned to the purpose of the organization.

I define the "right" people as those who:

1. Align to the purpose, or why, of the organization
2. Fit the values of the organization
3. Are highly capable in their respective roles
4. Create diversity and positive energy on the team

Remarkability can't happen without having the right people. Let's look at how to get, keep and develop the right people.

Determine the Structure

As part of the output from your research in the early days, you will get a sense of the organizational structure that currently exists, and the one that you will want to have in place. Some leaders may wish to keep the structure that is in place, while others may see opportunities for consolidation, redistribution or alignment to their purpose and brand to better achieve remarkability.

Factors to consider in a structure decision include efficiency, agility, empowerment, alignment of mandate and function, customer/member experience, cost centres, and your newly established purpose.

The structure will have to work effectively for you to achieve your purpose, but it must also be effective from an operating and performance standpoint. It should be agile, nimble and lean, capable of responding to shifting needs and preferences of customers and members or adapting to changes in the environment. Rigid structures and entrenched silos make responses to change and opportunities difficult to realize. Keep it simple, lean, relatively flat and dynamic, and structured so that teams can work together to achieve an outcome that is about value for the customer, not about protection of internal silos.

Deciding on the optimal structure may take some time as you see the organization in action and evaluate its performance. Rushing into making structural changes is not recommended because it can create upheaval in the team and is difficult and complex to undo. Therefore, take an appropriate amount of time to get it right. Having said this, if you've had a structure in place for some time and are not seeing the results that you want, you will have to question whether the people or the structure (or potentially both) is the root cause.

It's important to avoid fitting the structure to the people or skills that exist in the organization. I am now not a fan of creating roles to fit people's skill sets, expertise or interests if they are counter-productive or misaligned to the core of the organization. I once fell victim to this trap and devised a role that was an attempt to match the skills of an individual and the needs of the organization versus what you should always do—identify what you need and then find the right people. My approach failed miserably. The reality is that the role didn't align to what we really needed in the organization, which was a focus on member engagement and value. Neither the individual nor the role still exist in the organization.

Start at the Top

I recall very early on in my time at the Calgary Chamber an appointment with Michelle Berg, President and CEO of elevated HR, who at the time was a stranger to me, but is now a friend and advisor. She came to tell me that, as an HR advisor, she could help me, as a new leader, create a great team. Her first, and to this day most memorable, piece of advice: start at the top.

While obsessing about the fit of each new hire is a role for the CEO (see later in this chapter), the most important thing you can do as a CEO is hire the right people in the top leadership and management roles. Why? Because if you hire great people in senior leadership roles, you can generally trust them to hire great people under them.

How will you know what kind of person to hire on your leadership team? It depends on your style and what you want. There are countless theories, frameworks, books and models about leadership—and I encourage all leaders to expose themselves to as many as possible to find their own approach—but the reality is that leaders aren't born but made. Therefore, as you develop your own leadership style (as discussed in Chapter 2), you will naturally gain a greater understanding of the kind of team and the kind of leaders that you want to work with you and for you.

As a CEO, the people that I look for to be part of my leadership team are all the "right" kind of person as described at the beginning of this chapter. They complement me, they challenge me, they demonstrate effective and ethical leadership characteristics, are looking to grow and develop, they are highly capable in their respective fields and are on board with the purpose and my vision. With that kind of combination, you can expect them to make good hiring choices and that, when it comes to the final interview with you, most candidates will not disappoint.

The importance of solidifying a strong top team is reinforced by Patrick Lencioni in *The Four Obsessions of an Extraordinary Executive*. He describes four disciplines that executives should adhere to, with the first being to build and maintain a cohesive leadership team. Finding the right people at the top is the first step towards achieving a highly focused, cohesive and performance-oriented team.

The building of a high-performance leadership team is essential to the success of your Remarkability Agenda. In hiring your direct reports, you need to be focused and demanding. I made too many mistakes early on about wanting to be liked versus focusing on results (a key mistake as described by Patrick Lencioni in *Five Temptations of a New CEO*) and I paid for that in poor hires or promotions to the leadership team. I put people in roles they should not have been in. I was swayed and intimidated by big personalities and felt that I was not up to the tough conversation on underperformance. I let some people lead me to believe that they were doing an adequate job and that they had everything under control when they didn't. These were the errors of my inexperience—but failure and error are the best teachers. Over time, and with increased experience, and a desire to not repeat past mistakes, I hired better people, got past wanting to be liked, and focused on getting the job done.

Take the time to find the right people; it will be a major determinant in achieving remarkability. If your gut tells you someone doesn't feel right, don't hire them. If you don't think they can cut it, don't hire them. If you think your personalities will clash, don't hire them. But if you think they will constructively challenge you, deliver results, add new thinking and skills to the team, be curious, be effective leaders themselves, fit the values, be accountable, amplify the purpose and overall blend in with the rest of the team, then hire them. It isn't just about hiring slow, it's about doing the right kind of hiring to ensure you get the right kind of person on your team.

Building a Leadership Operating System

Team effectiveness doesn't just happen. It gets embedded, often through the systems, approaches and processes installed by the CEO. How a team works together, produces results, how they engage with their colleagues and direct reports, and their collaborative capacity is what I refer to as the "leadership operating system":

1. The accountability system within an organization's leadership hierarchy
2. The coaching and performance review model
3. The team's spirit or level of functionality and cohesion

A leader should ensure that they not only create and follow an operating system, but that they train and instill it in their senior leaders—people who will have to implement and use the system with their own staff.

The accountability system is a mixture of the CEO's leadership style and the systems that they put in place. A CEO will need to be highly disciplined to ensure that they establish an expectation and culture of accountability—that people will do what they say they will do, when they say they will do it, and that they will take responsibility for their achievements and failures. That is to be modeled from the top by the CEO and is to be reinforced through values and value-based systems such as coaching, performance reviews, monitoring performance, deadlines, progress and deliverables in regular meetings or intervals, and by holding people to account for their adherence to that. It is often tough cop and tough love, but organizations don't get anywhere without accountable leaders who then hold their teams to account.

A coaching approach should be taken to ensure meaningful conversations happen that lead to improvement. These coaching discussions should be held with direct reports on at least a quarterly basis in line with reviews but should also be held at the request of the staff, or before and after a moment of performance such as a report, presentation or event. More on this later in the chapter.

Once someone has performed, or has made progress against their goals, the performance should be assessed. The performance review process, discussed later in this chapter, is the system through which the organization ensures that people are living the corporate values, set goals, and regularly check in on those goals; it also ensures that a performance review is undertaken regularly to provide feedback on the achievements and shortcomings of staff members. This process helps staff grow and develop in their roles and expand their skill sets.

After your leadership team is in place, make sure that team is strong and nurture a strong team spirit. This team spirit represents the functionality and cohesion of the team in terms of its ability to trust, hold each other to account and embrace respectful and constructive conflict. Such a team is free of dysfunction and is a highly effective, collaborative and productive unit. It is one that enables good healthy collaboration, conflict, debate, and shared achievement which are vital to a remarkable organization. It takes effort and work; don't just slam a handful of people together and expect it to work out. Team dynamics will take time, effort and adjustment from everyone.

A variety of activities can help to maintain a healthy team spirit. Annual retreats that feature a combination of planning, digging into big topics, and team building activities are an excellent way to bring people together. As a team, learn a new skill, take on a challenge, share a meal or get some exercise together.

Create the space for debate, discussion, and creative conflict. A great place to start is by having each member complete a communication or behavioral profile. At the Calgary Chamber we implemented the DISC personality profiling system. Of all the tools available (e.g., Myers-Briggs), I have found DISC to be the best and most predictive of people's interaction and communication preferences. We shared each person's profile with them, their supervisor and their team. DISC enables a better understanding of how people interact, what stresses them out, how they process tasks and information, and what is most important to them when communicating. It can help team members to understand why people may face difficulties or conflicts when trying to work together. Every one of the staff and new hires at the Calgary Chamber undergoes a DISC profile.

Share the profile results with each other and then discuss how each person likes to engage and communicate. Enable discussions at meetings and sessions that allow for disagreement and conflict that can surface differing perspectives and ideas. A way to make this happen is to go through the process that Patrick Lencioni delineates in *Five Dysfunctions of a Team*; it helps teams get to a highly trusting and effective place together. You can use the accompanying workbook and the author's many recommended activities and team-building exercises to get past the dysfunctions.

Spending time together as a leadership team is also important. This is above and beyond the "work" but extends to each member as an individual. I have seen great relationships form when we work together on a team-building project such as outdoor survival skills or getting a meal together where we don't talk about work. Finding out what is important and inspiring to each member of the team will enable you to bring that team closer together. I also found ways to thank them individually and as a team, such as at board meetings. Once a year I would also host them and their spouses/partners for a dinner at my home to show my appreciation for their work and the support of their partners.

Individually, I would give them each a small gift and thank you note twice a year, at Christmas and our June retreat. These small gestures of appreciation can help to build the relationship and ensure that they know you value and appreciate the work, time and dedication that they are bringing to the role.

A Rigorous Approach to Hiring the Right People

After experimenting with many different approaches, I have found that a values-based approach to finding, keeping and developing the right people is the most effective. Chapter 6 outlined values and how to develop them for your organization, because they are highly important in the achievement of remarkability. Why? Because, in addition to your purpose, your values are a critical ingredient to finding, keeping and developing the right people.

The recommended approach is rigorous, but it works. Throughout the years that I have used it, it has consistently delivered the best performing people, the lowest turnover rates and the fewest conflicts in terms of performance and fit in the organization.

Working with our friends at elevated HR, the values-based approach that we used successfully is as follows:

1. Update the job description and post the role.

2. Collect and screen resumes based on a set of established skills or capability criteria.

3. Conduct a telephone interview with potential candidates focused on competencies and skills.

4. Ask candidates to complete a technical assessment to help the hiring manager determine if they can "do the job." This assessment may take the form of a report, an analysis, a presentation or helping at an event.

5. Candidates undergo a community interview with 2-4 members of the team who ask questions about the candidate's values and alignment to organizational values.

6. Candidates go through a detailed values interview with the HR advisor and hiring manager.

7. Candidates complete a DISC profile and references are checked.

8. The final one or two candidates meet with the CEO for a final values and fit interview.

9. The successful candidate is hired—or the process continues if the CEO vetoes the choices.

This is the process that was used for every role in the organization. You will likely want to use your HR department for this, or an external HR advisor if you don't have internal HR resources.

As CEO, it is important that you interview everyone if possible. There are stories of top executives like Larry Page, Jeff Bezos, Elon Musk and others who, even as their companies grew larger, still interviewed everyone. Why? Because adherence to the values and protection of the culture was vitally important to them. And while you hire great people to work beneath you on the leadership team, the entire organization is under your leadership and you want to ensure that everyone is the right fit.

This rigorous approach is validated by Patrick Lencioni in *The Four Obsessions of an Extraordinary Executive,* and specifically discipline four, which is "Reinforce organizational clarity through human systems." Through rigorous hiring and performance management, an organization's culture and high-performing nature can be created and maintained.

On occasion, you will encounter a candidate that has made it all the way to the final interview with you, the CEO but you do not support them. Don't be afraid of vetoing that hire. If your gut is telling you something is off, listen to it. You are probably right.

In the end, despite best efforts, hiring is a crapshoot. You get a small insight into a person, typically only hear positive endorsements, and never really get to see them in action under normal work conditions. It is a roll of the dice.

Despite best efforts and processes, I've still gotten it wrong. But if I really ask myself the question why, it's usually been because we skipped a step or brushed over a gut feeling. Perhaps we were in rush. Perhaps it had taken a long time to hire and this really was the best of all the candidates. And let's face it, you only get a small insight into a person during an interview. That said, I believe that implementing the above hiring process will increase your chances of success.

The Leader's Discipline: Coaching and Performance Assessment

One thing I have found throughout my career, primarily through experience, is that as someone progresses up the leadership ladder they are typically promoted based on their capability and skill in their role. But suddenly, they are responsible for the oversight, coaching, development and assessment of people who report to them. That is a completely different skill and side of our nature than the skills we have in our occupation. Suddenly, people are responsible for the growth, development, motivation and well-being of other people and no one has taught them how to do this. The ability to be good coaches, mentors and leaders is not innate. It must be learned and developed. It is a large part of the leadership skill set and a strong leadership operating system.

A key part of any leader's role is ensuring that your team are working on what they are supposed to at the level you need them to, but also that they are progressing in their goal achievement, work output and skill development.

I am a subscriber to the practice of regular goal-setting and performance assessments; at the Calgary Chamber, we did this quarterly. At the beginning of each quarter, all staff would set their goals. The individual's quarterly goals were tied to the departmental plan within which they worked and included personal professional development goals. At the end of each quarter, we would conduct reviews to assess performance against the goals, living the values, and other job and growth-related issues.

We used a coaching approach in our quarterly reviews that was modelled on a framework built by Ian Chisholm at Roy Group and their Leader's Discipline program which treats feedback as a gift that is specific, real-time and non-judgmental. Coaching and feedback should be tied to a performance moment or output. That is why quarterly assessments work well, for you can frame reviews and assessments around more discrete goals or outputs versus the traditional annual review, which is extremely cumbersome and suffers from recency syndrome as supervisors are often challenged to recall anything earlier than three months anyways.

For the reviews, individuals fill out their self-assessment indicating their achievement of goals (yes/no), living the values (yes/no), and answering the following questions:

- What they felt worked well and that they should be recognized for
- What was tricky and needs improvement
- What they will do to improve, how we will know they have improved, and what they need from management to help with improvement

Supervisors review this form and then answer each of the above three items from their own perspective. The team member and supervisor sit down and discuss their respective views and come to a shared understanding of where recognition should be given, where improvement is needed and how that will be achieved. This all blends into the creation of the next quarter goals in terms of work requirements but also personal development.

Additionally, if there is a moment of performance that needs to be addressed or supported, staff can discuss expectations, ideas and plans with their supervisor, and then ask for feedback after that moment of performance. If a supervisor wants to provide unsolicited feedback after a performance moment, then they are encouraged to do so, even outside the confines of a quarterly performance review.

This approach works extremely well. It helps people see themselves in the bigger picture, it keeps work flowing, reduces the amount of work crammed into the final quarter of the year due to procrastination, and creates an opportunity for a real-time dialogue on how things are progressing in terms of an individual's skill set and performance.

This approach is also key to instilling a high-performance culture. The consistency and routine of setting goals and being evaluated emphasizes the importance of achievement, completion and growth. I partially credit this approach to the stability and consistency of the Calgary Chamber's high-performance culture.

Rewards and Recognition

According to Daniel Pink in *Drive: The Surprising Truth About What Motivates Us,* people are motivated by three things: purpose, autonomy and mastery. I've found that people also appreciate recognition and rewards. For high performers who want to work for a bigger purpose, "rewards" are larger than merely financial rewards; in fact, financial rewards rarely drive people who work for values-based, purpose-driven organizations.

There are many ways that organizations can recognize and reward people that align to values and a purpose. Find ways to engage the whole team and make rewards and recognition something that isn't just the leadership team's responsibility.

- Recognize value champions or heroes at weekly staff meetings, for colleagues who have stepped up above and beyond, truly living the values in the past week.

- Use an online recognition platform (we used Kudos and found it was a great tool), that enables all staff to recognize their colleagues. With these tools, each staff member can distribute an amount of kudo credits to their colleagues each month based on how they demonstrated living the values or going above and beyond. Employees can then cash in kudo credits for gift cards or experiences.

- Deliver a personal note, recognition or special lunch to a colleague in appreciation for their work and adherence to the values.

Recognition and team building is also a very important part of leadership. Whether it is a regularly scheduled social outing, impromptu drinks after work or an annual year-end celebration, taking the team out to say thank you is something that will help create a connection between them and the organization.

I am not a celebrator by nature, so I often don't naturally do things to celebrate achievement and accomplishment. For me, it has been helpful to have members on my leadership team who are more naturally inclined to celebrate, or to schedule things regularly, for if left to my own devices I am certain that I would neglect celebration more than I should. Leaders need to be there for their teams to show appreciation and build trust so that the team will be there when they are needed the most. Consider appointing a Social Committee that can help with planning regular events to build camaraderie and have some fun.

Taking the Team Temperature: Staff Surveys

You have read it here and you will hear it from many people: the CEO job is the loneliest in the office. Few people tell you what you want to know, and many are polite and reserved, treating you more as a tiger about to pounce than as a colleague. While some leaders can build an environment of total openness and honesty amongst all colleagues, I believe that is the exception rather than the rule. I'm not saying that you should expect to be treated as though you were Genghis Khan, but it is highly likely that, as CEO, you'll never <u>really</u> hear what you want and need to hear and will have a difficult time keeping your finger on the true pulse of the team dynamic, particularly in larger offices.

A staff survey can help you overcome these constraints. This confidential annual survey lets people provide feedback on specific elements of the organization, their role, their environment and their enjoyment of their work. It often identifies opinions that would not have been uttered publicly or even privately to a person higher up the organization chain.

Be prepared for some venting and some griping. This is all part of the process and is healthy, if it is done in a productive and positive manner. Be prepared for some negative feedback and comments. But treat that feedback as a gift that will help you make the work experience more enjoyable and positive to retain your good people. Reinforce the positive feedback by continuing to do those things that people like and develop a plan to address those things that people suggest need improvement or have concerns about.

The results of the survey and the recommended actions should be shared with all staff so that they know their views are taken seriously and are valued. Providing the results and the action plan shows that this exercise, but more importantly their views, are important to you.

At the Calgary Chamber we used questions developed by Gallup for a simple but comprehensive overview of working at the organization. This survey uses a strict Yes/No response to a variety of statements. I prefer the Yes/No approach as it forces people to have an opinion. Sliding scales often create zones of uncertainty and neutrality and can be hard to work with in terms of taking action. The definiteness of a Yes or No enables leaders to act with some certainty.

Expect Resistance

Not every moment of team building will be rosy, and in fact for a new leader the whole thing can be quite challenging. This is particularly the case for the team that you inherit. While many people will be excited to see a new leader, some may be wary, concerned, scared and even resistant to the directions you want to take and the changes that you want to make. Therefore, you need to approach the team issue with sensitivity, clarity and objectivity.

In your assessment of the organization, you will get a good sense of what you have from a talent perspective. Do you have skilled people? Are they team oriented? Are they aligned to organizational values and purpose? Do they harbor any frustrations or animosity? Are they motivated and accountable? Are they deadweight? Can they be brought around? These are the kinds of questions you will need to ask yourself to develop a picture of the team that you inherit.

Some will support you. Others will actively undermine you. Be especially cautious of those that sought the job you recently won. Productive relationships between those who lost out on the competition and those who won it are rare, and you may wish to make changes in those roles quickly to avoid impairing the performance or team dynamic.

You will need to outline organizational changes, particularly in structure and role, with sensitivity to those involved and impacted, but also to those left out of, or negatively impacted by, the changes. Articulating to people why changes are happening and what they mean is critical; your team needs to see the rationale for the change, and why it will be better for them in the end. Working with an HR resource to help address organizational change is a valuable expense in the early days to help manage the emotional and interpersonal impacts of change and of building the right team.

I faced many challenges in trying to build the right team. I made a lot of rookie mistakes, largely because, contrary to what Patrick Lencioni advocates in *The Five Temptations of a CEO*, early on I chose being liked over holding people accountable or making tough decisions. I kept people around too long, and put people in roles they couldn't succeed in. I created organizational change that fit the person, not the purpose, and didn't hold people accountable enough. All of this resulted in poor organizational performance in my early years.

Needless to say, I learned a lot from that experience and now have a simple people and team philosophy:

1. Get the structure right, but don't be afraid to change if needed.
2. Hire the "right" people and do all you can to keep them.
3. Create the conditions to enable them to do their best work.
4. Work hard but make it enjoyable and engaging.
5. Hold them highly accountable.
6. Set goals and review performance regularly.
7. Hire slow based on rigorous process, and fire fast based on values, performance and accountability.
8. If your gut is telling you something, listen to it.
9. Give people meaningful work and opportunities to grow and develop.
10. Ask and listen.

Resource Kit

Ask This—Diagnostic 4

(You can complete all diagnostic questions from each chapter online at www.makingremarkable.com)
Use a rating of Yes=1, No=0. A score of 80% or better indicates that you are likely remarkable in that element.

1. Structure, People and Hiring
   a. Is your current organizational structure what it needs to be to achieve remarkable results?

b. Is your team made up of at least 80% the "right people" (i.e., align to the purpose and values, highly capable, diverse and positive)?

c. Is the organization free of toxic inter-personal dynamics?

d. Do you use a rigorous, values-based approach in your hiring?

e. Do you assess how staff live the values and purpose in performance reviews?

2. Leadership Team and Operating System

a. Do you have a solid leadership team made up of the "right people"?

b. Does the leadership team have a culture of accountability, and regularly hold each other accountable?

c. Is there a strong level of trust amongst the leadership team that enables the creation of strong relationships?

d. Does your leadership team engage in constructive conflict with each other to create better results and outcomes?

e. Does the leadership team do things together to get to know each other, such as retreats, dinners, lunches, activities and spend time together?

3. Goal Setting and Reviews

a. Does every staff member set goals at least semi-annually that are aligned to organizational targets and include personal development goals as well?

b. Do goals incorporate learnings and outcomes of previous reviews in order to help staff to grow and develop?

    c.   Do you hold performance review sessions at least semi-annually with staff to review goal achievement and areas for development?

    d.   Do all staff know how their work, targets and goals fit into the bigger picture of the organization's overall targets and objectives (i.e., they have a line of sight between what they are working on to the overall organizational targets)?

    e.   Do you truly hold staff accountable for poor performance (i.e., some kind of development implication or consequence)?

4. Coaching and People Development

    a.   Do all people responsible for staff oversight know how to be effective people leaders and good coaches for their direct reports?

    b.   Do your people managers and coaches use an approach that provides feedback on a real time basis, instead of waiting until a regular review cycle?

    c.   Do you provide opportunities for people to gain new skills on the job, such as expansion of responsibility, or supporting other parts of the organization?

    d.   Do you support/fund professional development for all staff?

    e.   Do at least 80% of your staff know what is expected of them at work, based on your regular staff surveys?

5. Rewards and Surveys

    a.   Do you have a rewards and recognition program that is tied to your values?

b. Are all staff able to recognize and reward their colleagues through formal or informal means?
c. Do you do an annual staff survey?
d. Do you share the results of the staff survey with the team?
e. Do at least 80% of your staff enjoy their work and feel a connection to your purpose and values, according to your survey?

Do This to be Remarkable

- Determine the structure that you need to be remarkable.
  - ○ You will have likely inherited an existing structure, so examine it, see it in action, test it and model out what you will need.

- Hire the "right" people and start at the top.
  - ○ Define what you need in terms of a team to fit the structure and find the right people that fit the values and purpose and will contribute positively – starting at the top.
  - ○ Use a rigorous, values-based people system – hiring, firing, rewards and advancement.
  - ○ Don't succumb to the temptations of new leaders. Do what is right for the organization.

- Create your leadership operating system.
  - ○ Know what is important to you in terms of how your team operates and functions. Set up rules, processes and approaches that will bring out the best in the people you have.
  - ○ Determine and implement your accountability system.

- ○ Nurture a team spirit – particularly within the leadership team

- Enable people to do their best work.
  - ○ Create a culture and approach to coaching and performance measurement that gives feedback and enables people to grow and develop.
  - ○ Reward and recognize people who perform and live the values
  - ○ Conduct annual staff surveys to enable people to provide feedback and suggestions in a safe and confidential manner.

- Expect resistance.
  - ○ Not everyone will be on your side. Prepare for that and plan in advance how you will respond.

- Develop your own people approach. This will help you be consistent and know what you want to build and establish as a team.

Review This

- BOOKS
  - ○ Daniel Pink, *Drive: The Surprising Truth About What Motivates Us*. Riverhead Books (2009).
  - ○ Cal Newport, *So Good They Can't Ignore You: Why Skills Trump Passion in the Quest for Work You Love*. Grand Central (2012).
  - ○ Patrick Lencioni, *The Five Temptations of a CEO*. Jossey-Bass (1998).
  - ○ Patrick Lencioni, *The Four Obsessions of an Extraordinary Executive*. Jossey-Bass (2000).
  - ○ Patrick Lencioni, *The Five Dysfunctions of a Team*. Jossey-Bass (2002).
  - ○ Paul Marciano, *Carrots and Sticks Don't Work: Build a Culture of Employee Engagement Built*

on the Principles of RESPECT. McGraw-Hill Education (2010).
- Beverly Kaye and Sharon Jordan-Evans, *Love 'Em or Lose 'Em: Getting Good People to Stay*. Berrett-Koehler Publishers (2014).
- Geoff Smart and Randy Street, *Who: The A Method for Hiring*. Ballantine Publishers (2008).
- Jason Fried and David Heinemeier Hansson, *REWORK*. Crown Business (2010).
- John Whitmore, *Coaching for Performance: GROWing People, Performance and Purpose 5th Ed*. Nicholas Brealey (2017).
- Daniel Coyle, *The Talent Code: Talent Isn't Born. It's Grown. Here's How*. Bantam (2009).
- W. Timothy Gallwey, *The Inner Game of Work: Focus, Learning, Pleasure and Mobility in the Workplace*. Random House (2001).

- OTHER
  - https://discprofile.com/
  - www.roygroup.com

PLATFORM

Your Platform is essentially how an organization activates its Purpose and People, the way it creates value and how it goes to market based on the nature of your purpose and your target market. The Platform pillar is comprised of four elements:

1. Value proposition and business model
2. Strategy and plans
3. Digital and technology
4. Finances

Let's look at each one in turn.

CHAPTER 9: Platform: Value Proposition and Business Model

What is it?	Your value proposition is the product, program and/or service offering you provide to your target market, aligned to their needs and deemed valuable, that enables you to generate revenue. Your business model is how you go to market, price and provide the product, programs and/or services.
Why is it important?	Having a strong and refined value proposition and business model aligned to your customer needs and ability to pay is essential. Otherwise, you'll struggle for customers and revenue.
Where do you start?	• Understand your target market and their needs. • Understand the current value proposition. • Assess each for alignment, gaps and performance. • Refine and rationalize your target market, then refine your product and service offering.
Remarkable is:	• A well-defined target market • A regular program of engagement and research that enables understanding of target market needs and challenges • A value proposition that delivers solutions to the needs or challenges of your target market • A process for testing and refining product or serve offerings to improve the notion of value by your customer or member • A business model that enables you to deliver your value proposition effectively and profitably

"The value proposition is the reason why customers turn to one company over another. It solves a customer problem or satisfies a customer need." Alexander Osterwalder and Yves Pigneur[14]

I vividly remember many of the board meetings that I had early in my time at the Calgary Chamber. Many of them were spent with well-intentioned and enthusiastic discussion about what the Chamber should offer: wine tastings; scotch tastings; wine and scotch tastings; themed dinners; business buddy programs; networking mixers; membership drives; education sessions. The board was an amazing idea factory.

At first, I wanted to show that I was taking the guidance and advice of my board seriously, and so I launched some of the ideas that they had suggested. Not a single one worked. Why? Because I didn't make sure any of these things were what our members wanted, nor did we deliver them effectively. Further, we simply added to the product offering without asking ourselves what we should remove if we were going to add something new. And so, after several failed efforts, I began to dissect what creating a targeted and valuable value proposition truly meant.

A value proposition is essentially your offering – product, service, program or experience - in helping meet a need, and how you are uniquely positioned to do it better or differently than anyone else. At its core, a value proposition should be rooted in meeting an unmet need or desire, a job that needs doing or solving a business challenge.

The best and most successful businesses are built by meeting a need and thereby solving a customer problem—some kind of pain point that you can address through your offering. By identifying customer or member pain points and solving them in a better/unique/faster/cheaper way, you should (all else being equal) have yourself a value proposition and hence a viable business. But keep those two parts front of mind: it is about understanding and identifying needs AND addressing those needs. You can't deliver a product or service without first understanding what is needed.

The same thing goes for organizations, associations, chambers of commerce, and many non-profits. Whether your value proposition is advocating to elected officials for better business conditions, making it easy to contribute to a cause people feel passionate about, or helping a member maintain a credential in their chosen profession, every organization needs to develop a compelling value proposition. Without one, you will struggle to maintain and attract customers, members or donors.

The Value Proposition Process

Much like the whole process of transformation and becoming remarkable, establishing your value proposition is never a "once and done" type of exercise. It is an iterative, ongoing process to fine-tune the target market and match your offering to the needs of that market.

Organizations that are facing declining sales, customers or members have a value proposition problem. That was the case when I arrived at the Calgary Chamber. While a brand problem was our biggest issue, we had lost the battle by failing to define and know our target market, what their business issues were, and how we could deliver something to them that would make their business more successful.

Too many organizations have let their value proposition slip or erode through the belief that it is something they could just set and forget, or through a lack of the discipline needed to ensure that it is tightly aligned to a target market and a highly-defined need.

Regardless of the situation that has gotten you to this place, you as a leader must recognize that building *and maintaining* a compelling value proposition requires focus, attention, vigilance and discipline. It needs to be deployed, tested, evaluated, refined and supported regularly. The development and refinement process for a target market and value proposition is shown in the following diagram:

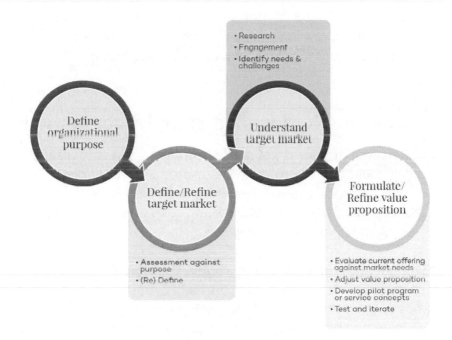

This chapter explores each of these key steps in creating your value proposition.

To keep a value proposition fresh and compelling, a leader and their team must always be scanning, understanding, assessing and evaluating the world around them to determine the relevance of the current proposition. Constant changes and adaptations to the value proposition are not just to be expected, they should be embraced.

If you're a CEO with a transformation mandate, you have likely inherited a value proposition that is stale, outdated and a large contributor to organizational underperformance.

Rebuilding the value proposition requires a deep dive into the needs and challenges of your target market. You cannot assess what you have, or what you need to change, without a clear understanding of your target market and their needs.

Define and Rationalize Your Target Market

Understanding your target market through active and regular engagement can help co-create your product and service offering by tapping into their exact needs and wants—and that should mean dedicated members and customers. But first you need to know exactly who they are.

You can't be everything to everybody. You shouldn't even try. The reality is that you need to routinely define and redefine your target market by assessing your purpose against a market segment and then determining if there is organizational ROI in what you offer.

Your purpose will, in many ways, significantly define your target market. Crafting your purpose creates the opportunity to foster a community—and that community is your target market. It also means that some other communities will be excluded. That's fine. In fact, it's necessary. Your value proposition analysis must include defining and then rationalizing your target customer or member market.

The first step in this process is to assess your new or revised purpose against your current target market to determine alignment. Do they fit together? Does the current target market align to the new purpose? If not, where is it misaligned? Does the purpose fit your target market, or does it have another more natural target market aligned to it? Does the purpose now remove certain segments of the target market naturally? Does it add new segments? Answering these questions will give you a definition of what your target market should be. This will now be tested using research and other data to ensure that it is the right fit.

The market research you will conduct (described later in the chapter), in combination with the assessment of your value proposition, should lead you to regularly ask this core question: Should we continue to serve this market segment?

Many organizations have caught themselves in a double trap: trying to be everything to everyone and trying to offer everything to everyone. The results include a misaligned or completely undefined target market, and a value proposition that is so broad and far-reaching that doing it well is impossible.

Because many organizations are loath to cut anything that could be perceived as value, they have continued to irresponsibly add programs and services without cutting anything, ultimately creating an untenable situation in terms of properly serving a specific target market and ensuring profitability. Regular rationalization – in other words, cutting - of what the organization delivers, and to whom, is necessary.

With a general sense of your desired target market in hand, you are ready for more rigorous rationalization. In *Race for Relevance*, Coerver and Byers provide a target market rationalization assessment template that provides many questions for leaders to ask about their market, such as changing engagement rates over time, trends, profile, market share and participation rate. I suggest you consult this valuable assessment tool.

By conducting a target market assessment, an organization can determine if there is in fact any value in continuing to serve a specific market. Some market segments may still make sense, but others—because of competition, technology, cost and a host of other factors—may not be worth pursuing as they represent a small percentage of customers or members or deliver very little in terms of financial ROI.

At the Calgary Chamber, we decided not to pursue start-up businesses as members. Through a combination of market research and our experience with startups, we realized that the resources we had available could not adequately address their biggest pain points or most intense needs: how to get started, advice on legal and accounting matters, and requests for countless meetings with potential clients. It was also clear that these small and early-stage companies had virtually no money to pay for a membership. Attempting to try and serve start-ups as paying members was causing frustrations on both sides of the transaction and so we made a purposeful decision not to continue to pursue them.

We were completely transparent about this decision and were comfortable with it because it freed us up to focus on market segments that we knew we could serve well. It was the right decision.

When you finish your target market rationalization you should have a clearly defined target market that aligns well to your purpose and resources. Now you are in good position to take the next step: understanding what your target market wants and needs.

Understand Your Target Market

Building or rebuilding a value proposition starts with one thing: deeply understanding your customer. Remember that a value proposition addresses a customer need, pain point or problem through aligning your offering with their need. If you don't know your customer well enough to truly understand their problems and pain points, you won't be successful in (re)crafting a meaningful value proposition. You've got to get inside their heads.

The value and import of good market research and engagement cannot be understated. It is vital to the successful leadership of today's remarkable organization. Extensive surveying of your customers, members, lapsed members, prospects and community will help inform your decisions on everything from value proposition to pricing and the performance of your team.

Here are some of the many things you will want to know about your customer:

- Current perspective (optimism or confidence?)
- Needs and preferences
- Outlook for their organization
- Investment or growth priorities
- Current pain points, challenges or problems in running or growing their organization
- Top barriers to growth
- Top opportunities for growth
- Preparedness for current and emerging trends
- Improvements needed to the public policy environment
- Feedback on current organizational performance:
  - Achievement of purpose
  - Current value proposition

- O Satisfaction and effectiveness of staff, investment, experiences, value proposition components etc.
- O Achievement of organizational purpose and mandate

If you don't do good market research, your decisions, investments and value propositions are built off hunches and gut feelings. Market research that is done well, and digs into the problems, needs, preferences and behaviours of customers or members, eliminates the costly risk behind hunch-based product and service development. Many a new CEO has looked at the historic performance of the organization that they have recently joined and has seen the past littered with defunct products and services launched on a hunch. Don't let this happen to you.

Conducting regular surveys, or other means of engagement, can provide insights into customer issues, pain points and problems. At the Calgary Chamber, we conducted semi-annual surveys with members and prospects. We asked about their biggest business challenges, barriers to growth, top areas of investment, new ideas they were considering, and what the next twelve months looked like for their business. Segmenting the data into profiles and personas let us see our members by market segment (size, lifecycle stage, etc.) and what the business challenges were for each segment. From there, we were able to assess our value proposition and its specific components against the top business challenges, and make decisions about what we needed to keep, cut and add.

As you explore the feedback of your customers and members, one very insightful question to explore is asking whether they feel that you are living up to your purpose and brand. If purpose is at the core of everything that you are as an organization, it really should be a key topic of engagement with your target market. A common mistake with organizations is that they say they are one thing, and then do, deliver and act in different ways, or even ways that contradict who they think or say they are.

Our board of directors suggested that we determine whether our members felt that we were living up to our purpose. We all agreed that our purpose was to help make our members more successful—but we had never asked them if we did that or not. We had assumed that membership sales and renewals were a good proxy for that data.

So, in 2016, we started asking that question directly: Did members feel that their membership with the Calgary Chamber helped make their business more successful? Yes or no? The first few times we asked the question, we got disappointing results; only 25% of members felt that their membership helped make their business more successful. We started digging for the rationale behind that low level of response. People weren't seeing the value they had wanted, and we also weren't effectively communicating back to them our work in terms of benefit. Through a combination of adjusting the value proposition and communicating better with our members, we were able to increase that figure to about 60% within 18 months. Member satisfaction grew as a result. It can be highly valuable to get good member feedback on whether you are truly living your purpose.

Another example of how research with your customer or target market can provide great insight is what we found in the spring 2017 business survey for the Calgary Chamber. In it, businesses had identified their top business need as securing new clients— they needed growth and new revenue. This need had jumped from mid-pack in previous surveys to become the top business issue by a margin of 2:1. We looked at our current value proposition and determined that we really had very little to offer in terms of helping a business find new clients. There were different events and products that could eventually lead to new clients if a member attended, but if a member was assessing their investment in the Chamber based on how many new clients they got, we would have a tough time living up to that. So, we began investing in programs, tools and events that would grow the chances of a member developing new business from their Chamber membership, including speed networking, referrals, and more curated networking based on digital member profiles.

There are other means of engagement (e.g., focus groups, one-on-one meetings and other structured and unstructured interactions) to collect data about your customer and members. These should augment, but never replace, a formal market research program. Unless your organization is a group of CRM power users, it is too easy for this other data collection to be poorly captured, stored and analyzable, leading to further decisions made on gut feel versus good data. Having said that, all data and insights gleaned from any interaction with a member, customer, or prospect should be recorded in some form (such as a CRM) for better understanding, targeting, sales, renewal and data mining needs.

Engaging and interacting with your target market as a team and staff is essential in helping keep the value proposition fresh. I always coached the Calgary Chamber team to get out and meet with our members and to understand what kept them up at night as business owners and leaders. This was so that we could keep the value proposition aligned to their needs and do our job better. In fact, this was so important to me that annually we would take all the staff on a member bus tour to visit a group of members at their place of business and learn more about what they do and to understand their biggest challenges. This was imperative in being able to give them value back in programs and services. Only by really knowing your customer's business challenges can you build a solid and compelling value proposition that will ensure repeat and renewed business.

As an organizational leader, you must understand your target market. You must understand what keeps them up at night. In fact, in all my years of working with businesses of all sizes, that was my standard question: what is keeping you up at night? That question enables an organization like a chamber to deliver a solution that will help them solve that problem or that takes that pain away.

And that, is value.

Asking those questions enabled us to come up with several programs at the Calgary Chamber. For example, I kept hearing from small and mid-sized private company owners and CEOs that they felt alone and didn't have anyone they could talk to about their challenges. They explored groups like EO and TEC but either didn't find a match or felt them too constraining. We did research and found the Peerspectives program out of the Edward Lowe Foundation. After looking into this program, we found that it was delivered in a similar peer learning approach but not in such a rigid and structured way. The CEO Peer Mentoring program we implemented 2013, based on the Peerspectives model, still helps solve an important pain point for a certain segment of business leader.

Digital Engagement

As an organization becomes more digitally savvy, it can begin using more sophisticated regular and real-time data collection for customer and member priorities, feedback on experiences, preferences, and emergent issues, including online surveys, social media, mining member spend and website patterns, or looking for use patterns and engagement as a customer.

Organizations that engage with their customers are actively building community and are more likely to deliver a product and service that fits the needs of their target market. Whether it is through dedicated channels of online community such as LinkedIn, Facebook or some other community engagement platform, these mechanisms need to be part of any organization's toolkit for better understanding its customer. Not only can they be used for engagement, but they are increasingly being used to co-create programs and services. Your community may be an excellent group to help shape and propose ideas that become part of your value proposition process laid out earlier in this chapter. They can be sought to help shape ideas, propose solutions and seek feedback—all digitally, and even supplemented with face-to-face. More and more solutions are being developed by people outside the organization because they are not tied to the conventions or approaches that create the immune system.

This is more advanced territory for many organizations, but it should be on the radar of any CEO who is looking to continually evolve the value proposition and deliver customer value.

Assessing Your Current Value Proposition

Once you have a firm understanding of your target market and their needs, preferences and pain points, it is time to assess the current value proposition for its suitability against those needs. To do so, you will need good data from your market research, as well as customer/member data from your programs and product offerings.

Ultimately, assessing the value proposition and its suitability is about aligning your customer/member needs and your product and service offering. Do your customers and prospects need what you're offering? Are they using it? Where are the gaps between what they need and what you're offering?

A CEO will need to dig into the data on customer segmentation, what programs and services have been used and at what rate, and how these programs and services are impacting the organization's bottom line and human resources.

For the world of associations and chambers of commerce, Harrison Coerver and Mary Byers have come up with an excellent matrix template to map your offerings and assess their effectiveness in meeting the needs of your customer or member. *Race for Relevance* provides a template for organizations to assess every part of their value proposition offering, by assessing how every product, program or service relates to purpose, life-cycle position, percentage of members or customers that use it, and financial performance (net income) amongst other metrics. You will see the usage of current programs and services and where you may want to increase or decrease resources.

The next step in (re)building your value proposition is to match your target market needs with the current value proposition to see if any needs are unmet. Here is a template and example for this kind of assessment:

Target Market Need (Derived from market research and engagement)	Existing Product or Service to Meet Need (Based on existing product and service offering)	Product or Service Performance (Derived from the assessment/matrix suggested in *Race for Relevance*)
Need 1	Product 1	Poor—redevelop or total overhaul—bring forward to Value Proposition Canvas
Need 2	No product or service—identified gap and opportunity for new product/service creation	N/A—bring forward to Value Proposition Canvas
Need 3	Service 3	Excellent—potential for growth
Etc.		

Based on the above example, this organization has the potential to better meet the needs of its customer or member. Need 1 is being met with a product, but it's performance is poor, therefore the product needs redevelopment or a total overhaul. Need 3 is being met with a service, and its performance is excellent, however, there is potential to grow and scale it.

The real opportunity lies with Need 2—currently unmet by the organization and ripe for the creation of a new product or service. Unmet needs are ripe for a product or service offering. Next steps here will be to assess if any other organizations are meeting this need and if you can compete, or if no one is offering anything, then there is potential for blue ocean. Take this opportunity forward through the Value Proposition Canvas and Business Model Canvas—which will be described later in this chapter—to validate and develop the right offering to meet the need. It should be noted that this step merely identifies that a need exists. The next part of the chapter will assist you in developing a potential program or service response to that need.

Key to successfully making a new offering work is to make sure you consider eliminating something that isn't working or is not meeting a need. If after completing the above matrix you have existing product and service offerings that have not been included as an offering to meet a need, consider that a flag. This means that you are offering something that is not meeting a need. That is a prime candidate for elimination—which will be discussed in the next section. Continually adding to the offering means you are at risk of spreading resources too thin. That will put the new offering and its success at risk.

Assessing your existing value proposition at both a high level and in component detail shows you the health of the current value proposition and its alignment and suitability to your organization's refined target market. This assessment should identify challenges, opportunities and insights into why customers/members are leaving or staying, or why the organization is feeling stale or outdated. The analysis will also reveal those areas (such as member renewals or net income) where the organization is achieving a net positive outcome, and those where they are losing out. Having this information in hand enables more informed and purposeful decisions to be made. The reality is that most CEOs have some degree of a stale or outdated value proposition with multiple product and service offering gaps that can be filled to meet target market needs and grow customer/member retention and sales.

Depending on the status of initiatives such as your rebrand or strategy efforts, you may have already begun an analysis of the value proposition. If not, you can do this assessment internally, or through a third-party advisor. The key is to use accurate and robust data from your current, lapsed or desired customer, and to be honest in assessing what is working and what is not.

Focusing Your Organization: Take Out the Scissors

Organizations must become leaner and more focused. To achieve this, they need to assess strengths, concentrate resources and ensure that they deliver only what they can do better or differently than another organization. This involves difficult decisions such eliminating some programs and services—but these cuts and streamlining make the organization more focused and eliminate waste.

Peter Drucker nailed it when he acknowledged that trimming is a critical element of pursuing new opportunities that will lead to growth. Just like pruning everything from trees to grape vines will enable the future grow back to be stronger and more robust. Organizations need to get into the practice of pruning. Drucker states: "the first step in a growth policy is to...decide what to abandon. To grow, a business must have a systemic policy to get rid of the outgrown, unproductive and the obsolete."[15] It is what he termed "purposeful abandonment."

A CEO must embrace a practice of "purposeful abandonment" to be able to really achieve remarkability. Too often—and chambers of commerce are particularly bad for this—organizations continually add to their value proposition without ever reducing what they offer. The result: resources that are spread more and more thinly across many activities that yield no ROI or market benefit. Purposeful abandonment is a critical part of any transformation and a CEO must have the courage to follow through with eliminating things that some people say they value, but in the end only meet the needs of a few and tax the limited resources of the organization.

In my time at the Calgary Chamber, we abandoned a number of activities but two stand out. First was our 7:15 Breakfast Networking Club, which was deemed by the founders and hard-core attendees to still be been "going strong" after 15 years. I attended a lot of these sessions and found that they didn't align well with our brand and purpose. Each participant gave a 90-second pitch to tell the others who they were and what they wanted in terms of a connection or contact. People then filled in paper referral slips. The whole experience just felt uncomfortable and old-school. Regular attendees complained that there were never enough new people attending who could become potential clients, and new attendees rarely returned because they never got any immediate business out of it (for some reason, members of chambers of commerce think there is an immediate link between joining and new business, and then leave when that doesn't happen!). From what I could see, we were a long way from "going strong." While some people told us that the 7:15 networking was their sole reason for maintaining membership, when we surveyed participants and members overall, it was found to yield virtually no benefit. We therefore purposefully abandoned it and focused our time and resources on more productive activities.

The second activity we abandoned was our annual swearing in of the board chair and fundraising dinner. Every January we held the President's Ball, during which we recognized the past chair, swore in the new chair, recognized volunteers, and conducted fundraising activities (like a silent auction). Having attended this event even before I became the President and CEO of the Calgary Chamber, I can attest that it was never overly exciting and felt too focused on us as a chamber. Because it didn't reflect our revised brand, which was focused on helping our members be more successful, I took the bold step of cancelling the event—even though it brought in about $100,000 net income. This was a painful hit financially, but it didn't align to our brand and few really enjoyed it. We redeployed and reimagined the activities and found alternative ways to raise the same amount of money through other events. Cancelling this event was more aligned to our brand and forced us to be more creative as to expanding our revenue stream.

(Re)Building Your Value Proposition

Once you have rationalized the target market and assessed the current value proposition, you must make any adjustments to the value proposition to create a leaner and more focused offering. The assessment outlined above will identify gaps for existing offering adjustment, new offering creation and areas to cut. You will need to think in terms of both creation and elimination.

Getting to a better offering requires you to (re)build the value proposition. I recommend the Value Proposition Canvas and the Business Model Canvas available through Strategyzer. These tools are open- and crowd-sourced tools used by some of the world's top companies to test and validate business offerings.

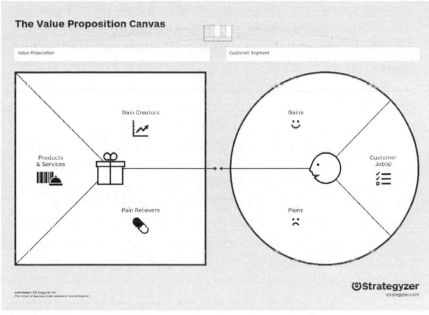

SOURCE: www.strategyzer.com

The Value Proposition Canvas offers a deeper dive into the Value Proposition and Customer Segment sections of the Business Model Canvas. Use it to find a match between customer jobs or pain points and requirements with your product and service offerings. At its core, it helps you create the best fit between what you offer and what your customer needs. It can help assess current offerings in your value proposition and suggest new offerings to address unresolved customer problems.

To get started, insert the data from your market research and internal data analysis on the customer segment portion of a Value Proposition Canvas, then put down your current and potentially new offerings on the value proposition portion of the Value Proposition Canvas.

(Re)building a value proposition will be the result of an iterative process of testing and conceptualizing offerings against the customer side of the Value Proposition Canvas. Working through a variety of potential product or service offerings against the customer job or pain points will help to determine the suitability of your value proposition and the need to adjust it to better meet customer needs. At this point you may want to do this yourself or bring in a consultant to help shape the potential program or service solution. In addition, your community and target market are also a great way to tap into new ideas to help co-create ways to address the pain points. Regardless of the approach, find ways to bring in new perspectives and new ideas to helping solve your customer or member pain points—the organization no longer is the sole source of great ideas.

At the Calgary Chamber, we used this iterative approach to refine the CEO Peer Mentoring program. Early versions were deemed to be too rigid and structured by participants when we surveyed them post-program, so we attempted to ease off on the structure. Subsequent efforts resulted in being not structured enough, so we reverted to somewhere in the middle; the program has remained in that state ever since.

We also used this approach with a Calgary Chamber offering called Ignite, an innovation accelerator meant to provide a toolbox for second-stage companies to innovate and find new revenue streams, customers or markets. We launched it in spring 2017 with an initial cohort of four companies who agreed to serve as our test market. We refined the product based on their feedback and launched cohort two with a revised approach. With further feedback and input from the second cohort, we refined and launched cohort three using an even more refined model. All of this was done in the span of just eight months and Ignite is now a thriving and dynamic program at the Calgary Chamber.

Depending on your organization you may need to develop a few Value Proposition Canvases to address individual customer segments or needs. This iterative process is necessary because of the degree of uncertainty that organizations live within, and the need to test concepts before making full- scale investments in them. Too many organizations have bet large sections of the farm on something that wasn't right for the time or hadn't been properly tested.

In rebuilding the value proposition, ensure that you approach the task from the right perspective—which is not to maximize revenue or achieve revenue growth. While you need to ensure that someone is willing to buy what you are selling, try asking your offering will address the pain points of your customers/members? How will you help solve their biggest problems? Then figure out if you can make money from it.

A value proposition based on the needs and pain points of customers will have far greater resonance and lasting power than one which is contrived through the lens of how it will make your organization successful. Some organizations build a value proposition on what they think will make them money without asking: is there anyone who will buy what we are selling?

A cautionary note; many organizations fall into one of two traps:

1. They launch something without adequately understanding their market or putting the right testing and feedback mechanisms in place.

2. They quit after one negative launch without iterating or adjusting to see if some modification would increase success.

Either of these situations results in offerings that are not aligned to customer needs, financial loss, missed opportunities or offerings remaining on the books for far too long. You risk using valuable resources or betting the farm on something that is unproven. Using an iterative approach increases your chances of success.

Once you have determined that there is a match between your current or future offering and a customer pain point or problem, you can finalize your Value Proposition Canvas with real, tested ideas and offerings. You now have an updated value proposition. From here it then needs to be built into your product line up and promoted in a way that speaks to the benefits and results that it will bring to your customer.

After that, further solidify your business model and determine how to effectively go to market by building out the rest of the Business Model Canvas, an open source tool for establishing a business model.

Value Proposition Disruption

In *Exponential Organizations,* Salim Ismail suggests that much of disruption to incumbent value propositions and business models comes from unbundling or re-bundling existing activities.

Chambers of commerce offer events, networking, business programs and advocacy. Some organizations are disrupting that model by offering single elements of that bundled value proposition; LinkedIn and Business Network International

(BNI), for example, provide global business networking. Executive education programs and online courses have disrupted traditional business programming. If all those organizations that have unbundled activities formed an alliance and offered what chambers of commerce offered, but at a fraction of the cost, that re-bundling would also pose a risk to chambers.

In essence, the real disruption to the association world is unlikely to come from one source, but from a multitude of sources and potential approaches. This is reflective of how wide and broad the value proposition of the traditional association world has become. It is clearly time to be more disciplined and focused to better stave off disruption.

The Business Model

Once you have landed on a refined and validated value proposition, with programs and services that evidence demonstrates will be sought after and paid for by your target market, you must solidify the business model. That means defining things such as activities, resources, channels, supply chains, and partnerships and, if you're using the tool, completing the balance of the Business Model Canvas.

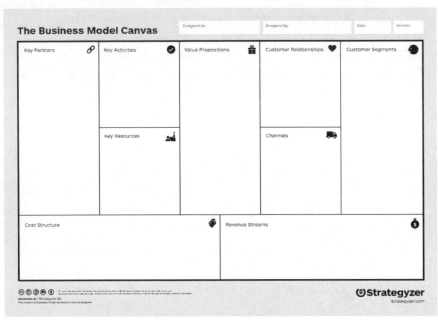

SOURCE: www.strategyzer.com

As you revise the business model, consider how it will be structured in terms of revenue stream: a dues-based model, a non-dues-based model, a hybrid, or newer structures (like a social enterprise model) if your organization can make them work. The business model should also reflect your brand and purpose; remember that your actions speak more loudly than your words.

Today's associations, and chambers of commerce in particular, are debating the future of the membership model, given that so much of what associations and chambers do is under competitive threat. Some chambers are experimenting with adjusted member models that blend large patron support, support for specific programs and value, and a broad-based "free" membership.

Another hotly debated feature is the tiered membership dues model, whereby memberships are packaged to offer increasing levels of benefits for higher price points. This is opposed to the fair share model in which all members received the same base benefits package, but larger companies or those with higher bank deposits are charged a higher rate.

The Calgary Chamber converted to tiered dues in 2012 and never looked back. The belief, still held today, is that charging (or penalizing from another perspective) a company more because it is larger or wealthier without any corresponding value improvement is not the right way to go to market. Therefore, we implemented a tiered member dues approach, with the help of internationally recognized chamber of commerce expert Kyle Sexton, to better provide increasing value to members willing to pay for additional value. It has worked well, and the organization continues to stand behind that decision.

Resource Kit

Ask This—Diagnostic 5

(You can complete all diagnostic questions from each chapter online at www.makingremarkable.com)
Use a rating of Yes=1, No=0. A score of 80% or better indicates that you are likely remarkable in that element.

1. Target Market and Customer Needs
    a. Do you have a tightly defined target market/customer/member?
    b. Was your target market reviewed and assessed in the last three years?

    c. Do you have active and regular means of understanding your customer, and their needs and perceptions (i.e., market research, focus groups, crowd sourcing, engagement and appropriate data tracking measures)?

    d. Do you have a means for staff to capture intelligence, such as in a database or CRM, on what they are seeing/hearing/learning from existing, past and future customers or members so that you can adapt your value proposition?

    e. Are at least 80% of your customers/members satisfied with the performance of your product, program or service, or the value they receive?

2. Value Proposition and Business Model

    a. Do you have an established value proposition?

    b. Have you ever completed a value proposition canvas, or updated your value proposition in the past three years?

    c. Have you completed, and acted upon, a product and service assessment for your organization within the past three years that identified where your programs and services are either over/under performing?

    d. Have you purposefully abandoned underperforming programs or services in the past five years?

    e. Have you ever built, launched and refined a program or service using a pilot project approach?

Do This to be Remarkable

- Don't be everything to everyone.
  - ○ Refine your target market to an effectively and capably serviceable group of people, members or customers. Spreading yourself too thin will lead to a lack of remarkability.

- Really know what keeps people up at night.
  - ○ Conduct thorough research on your members to understand their pain points, challenges and what keeps them up at night. Use this knowledge to deliver programs or services back to them so that you create a market opportunity and viable business.

- Test and iterate.
  - ○ When you have your target market and you know what their pain points are, develop a pilot to meet these needs and then test, seek feedback, refine and test again. Doing this over and over will create the best fit for your market in the shortest time with the least investment needed. Your target market will have great ideas of what you can do to help them.

- Use readily available tools.
  - ○ There are lots of tools to help in this process. Don't reinvent the wheel.

- Refine, refine, refine.
  - ○ Refine your value proposition and business model based on what your target market needs, feedback, your capabilities, your resources and what you can deliver.
  - ○ This process is iterative. You must always be looking, scanning and adapting to stay relevant and viable.

Review This

- BOOKS
  - Alexander Osterwalder and Yves Pigneur, *Business Model Generation*. John Wiley and Sons Inc. (2010).
  - Rita Gunther McGrath, *The End of Competitive Advantage*: *How to Keep Your Strategy Moving As Fast As Your Business*. Harvard Business Review Press (2013).
  - Eric Reis, *The Lean Startup: How Today's Entrepreneurs Use Continuous Innovation to Create Radically Successful Businesses*. Crown Business (2011).
  - Salim Ismail, *Exponential Organizations: Why new organizations are ten times better, faster, and cheaper than yours (and what to do about it)*. Diversion Books (2014).
  - Harrison Coerver and Mary Byers, CAE, *Race for Relevance: 5 Radical Changes for Associations*. ASAE The Centre for Association Leadership (2011).

- OTHER
  - *www.strategyzer.com*

CHAPTER 10: Platform: Strategy and Plans

What is it?	Strategies and plans are the pathways and roadmaps between your purpose and your results and between the present and the future. They provide the targets for your organization, as well as the steps needed to get there. Done well, these provide the framework to achieve remarkability and enable innovation, creativity and flexibility.
Why is it important?	Activity without direction, or established measure of success, is merely hobby. Targets and plans enable unifying actions, coordination and allocation of resources. Clear lines of sight between action and target are needed for an organization and its individual team members to achieve success and remarkability.
Where do you start?	• Assess existing strategies and plans for fitness and suitability. • Map out a process and framework for building your new strategy. • Initiate strategic conversations on the future realities facing your organization with key stakeholders and subject matter experts.
Remarkable is:	• A defining North Star aligned to your purpose • A simple strategy, no longer than three years in horizon which allows creativity and flexibility in execution • Clearly defined objectives and key results (OKR) and accountabilities • A clear line of sight from multi-year strategy to individual staff quarterly goals • A culture and mechanism/process to track, monitor and report performance

"Hope is not a strategy. Luck is not a factor." James Cameron[16]

We've all been there. That day of your life that you will never get back. The morning starts with trying to cobble together the vision and mission, followed by a SWOT analysis; the afternoon is spent developing goals using Post-It notes, and wordsmithing by committee. The board approves the bland, misguided and vague set of statements and directions for the next five years. And then no one looks at it again.

That's how strategic plans traditionally come to be.

These plans usually fail. And 99% of them suck. You need to do something different.

Strategy and Plans

Strategies articulate a future and a direction. Plans are a sequence of actions towards an end state. They're similar, but they're different. Strategies are about the future, using a broad-based conceptualization of what you aim to achieve, while plans are detailed lists of actions. Strategies typically span multiple years, while plans are better developed for shorter periods of time or discrete activities. Both are necessary for the right reasons and under the right applications.

This chapter is essential to defining where you want your organization to go, how you will know when you get there, and how to get your team aligned and focused on their part in achieving the destination. As a leader, you must clearly define what your remarkable organization looks like and provide the line of sight to getting there.

Equally essential is the continued mindset of constant change and adaptation, and the ability to be nimble and responsive to changing times. Even with strategy, it should never be a set and forget approach. Evaluating the world around you, understanding what is likely to happen next, and adjusting your organizational strategies, plans and actions are all essential. This chapter covers newer and more lightweight approaches to strategy and planning and makes the whole process of building and executing an organizational strategy much simpler compared to those seemingly endless days wasted in retreats.

Before we begin, let's look at some of the challenges and criticisms of traditional strategic planning.

Criticism of Traditional Strategic Plans

There has been much push back lately about "strategic planning." It is, in essence, an oxymoron. You can't identify a future or end state target (strategy) down to the level of knowing the exact actions (planning) you will use at each stage of the route to achieve the future target. One precedes the other; they cannot be created as a unified structure. Too much is changing too quickly these days to be able to map out a five-year organizational strategy and expect to identify the key actions needed over those five years. In fact, many organizations have switched from a five- to a three-year strategy—and even that feels too long, given the pace of change. An organization shouldn't put itself at risk by committing to a half-decade plan that might be totally irrelevant in six months. In *Exponential Organizations*, Salim Ismail proclaims, "death to the five-year plan" and suggests that the "only solution is to establish a big vision, implement a one-year plan (at most) and watch it all scale while course correcting in real time."[17]

Criticism also has been levelled at multi-year strategy processes on the grounds that they develop the future by looking at the past. Past performance. Results that have already occurred.

Experiences of previous years. Trends that have been shaped by the past. It's no way to build a forward-looking organization.

Traditional strategic plans also tend to be very "bulky," with a lot of elements: vision, mission, goals, strategies, objectives, actions, leads, timelines, etc. The process involved in creating such a massive structure is so time consuming and cumbersome as to render it almost useless. I don't know about you, but I have often struggled to split the hair of a strategy and objective, all the while realizing that it is largely irrelevant.

Another approach used in strategic planning is called "scenario planning"; it was pioneered by Pierre Wack of Royal Dutch Shell back in the 1970s and widely published a decade later. Since then, it has been used in a variety of ways but has not caught on as widely as the traditional strategic planning process, due largely to the size and complexity of its process.

Scenario planning requires that several strategy paths be considered, with actions proposed to address those different scenarios. As time unfolds, the organization implements the actions of the scenarios that seem to be playing out. The benefit of this process is that the organization can be ready for most of the scenarios and thus able to adapt and respond.

The reality with scenario planning is that it is time consuming, extensive and requires much analysis and development. It can be difficult, if not impossible, to predict what variables and factors to adjust in the different scenarios—you can spend a lot of time on situations that may never occur and may miss scenarios that do occur. While some swear by it, I have found it to be simply too complex for the organizations I have led.

That said, scenario planning has made a positive contribution to my own strategic work in that it has encouraged me to question assumptions and beliefs. What if this thing that I believe is true is in fact not true or at some point ceases to be true? What if this assumption is no longer valid? As a former chamber executive in a city that depends heavily on the oil and gas sector, I can tell you that we became good at challenging long- and widely-held assumptions.

A final criticism of strategic plans in general is that there is too little engagement of the board of directors. The board, while the governing body, is also responsible for ensuring that the organization establishes a dynamic strategy and ensures leadership is making progress towards achieving it. In my experience lately, boards are not demanding that organizational leadership demonstrate how their current efforts and activities are moving towards the achievement of their purpose and their longer term targets. Many boards do not ensure broad engagement in the creation of the strategy. Most boards approve a purpose and/or a strategic plan, but then assess only annual performance. Or they only review progress to purpose or long-term targets when the strategy is near completion and it is time to create a new one.

Boards need to be more engaged in assessing organizational leadership and holding them accountable for achieving long-term objectives and targets. Boards should require annual reporting on progress towards longer-term measures as well as the larger organizational purpose so that the temptation to be drawn into short-termism is reduced.

What's Really Important in Strategy and Plans

As noted above, the traditional strategic plan is very bulky in its articulation of myriad components, many of which are broken down so minutely that arguments ensue about what is a strategy and what is an objective. In other words, they are cumbersome and a time suck.

At their core, assuming they are built oriented around your purpose, strategies need to lay out just three key things:

1. Where your organization wants to go
2. How you will know when you get there
3. Who is accountable for making sure you get there

That's it.

Why just that? For many reasons. First, in developing a strategy, or even an annual business plan, it's hard to identify well ahead of time the approach or specific actions that will be best suited to achieving an outcome. I have often found, even with a one-year business plan, that the approach we thought we would use when we built it turned out not to be the best approach when it came time to implement or activate. Or something changed. Or a new version of a technology was released and created a new option or opportunity. Whatever the reason, I've changed course many times within the span of a few months. Trying to dictate what to do and how to do it before all the facts are available is rather pointless.

Second, the people that you've hired are smart. All they really need is an understanding of where the organization is heading (purpose and objectives), what the targets are (key results), what they are responsible for (accountability), and how their work fits into that direction and outcome (line of sight). From there, they can figure out the best path and actions for hitting those targets.

Another benefit of not locking down your plans with excessive specificity too far out: it sparks the creativity of your team. Too many plans are structured so that people's activities or roles are dictated to them. They stress activity more than outcome and they eliminate the opportunity for leaders and team members to be creative in their approach to achieving a set target. It's far better to set a target and then let a competent and experienced person determine the best approach to achieving that target. Plans and strategies that dictate approach reduce excitement and incentive to doing things in new and better ways.

At the Calgary Chamber, we set a five-year strategy for 2013-17. We achieved much of what we wanted to achieve earlier than planned, and some things had become irrelevant due to the changing demands of our members. Therefore, we cut the five-year strategy short and built a new, three-year strategy for 2016-18. Even before the end of 2017, it felt like a two-year strategy would have been better—again, a result of the way our thinking evolved and shifted as time, experience, and external forces led us to consider different and new ways of doing things.

The method that I now prefer is one in which an organization establishes a North Star (which is the defining performance measure that demonstrates the value that your customers are getting from your product or service—so, no, it isn't revenue or profit, something more like retention, satisfaction or willingness to recommend, or even improvement in customer/member performance), a few longer-term objectives, targets (i.e., a maximum of three years out) and accountabilities without a lot of detailed implementation structure, and then builds annual plans that align work to achieving those targets. By regularly monitoring performance of key results and metrics, the organization can adjust tactics and even the value proposition, business model or delivery vehicles if things are off track, or if the world changes.

The above approach that I prefer is reflective of the Objectives and Key Results (OKR) method developed by Andrew S. Grove at Intel; his book, *High Output Management*, is an excellent resource if you want to learn more. The OKR method has now become the de facto operating system for Silicon Valley and the startup community, and is sufficiently effective and lightweight, yet impactful, that it is being adopted by many different types of organizations.

OKR has become such a well-adopted approach because it recognizes the failings of inflexible multi-year plans but also provides enough direction that an organization can rally behind it. As Salim Ismail puts it in *Exponential Organizations*, "OKRs are about focus, simplicity, short(er) feedback cycles, and openness."[18] He further clarifies the nature of OKRs[19]:

- Objectives are the dream and strategic imperatives; Key Results are the success criteria.
- Objectives are qualitative; Key Results are quantitative.
- Objectives should feel ambitious and uncomfortable, as they represent a stretch for the organization.
- Key results should be assigned to a specific person or department for accountability.

The OKR method is essentially structured around two questions:

1. Where do we want to go as an organization? (Objectives: qualitative)
2. How will we know we are getting there? (Key Results: quantitative)

OKRs can be built for multi-year or annual purposes, and then broken down by quarter to get more specific. People accountable for a specific KR then develop actions or to-do lists that will achieve that specific KR so that teams can be tasked, and cross-team collaboration established.

This approach creates simplicity, structure and specificity as to where the organization is going, how it will measure success and who is accountable for certain metrics. It is lightweight in that there are few pieces to it. It enables real-time creation of action plans given that they are often created for specific quarterly KRs. Therefore, work plans reflect both the information known at the time and the available resources, and do not depend on prognostication about what someone thinks will work an entire year, or more, out.

A Caution Against Short-Termism

While I believe that the best approach nowadays in a time of significant change and disruption is to stay nimble, flexible and not overly committed to long-term strategies, I will say unequivocally that leaders and organizations still need to stay focused on the long-term.

This sounds like a paradox, I know. But let's break this down.

You can still be focused on the long-term while being flexible and oriented toward short-term strategy. I differentiate between long-term strategies and long-term outcomes. Long-term *strategies* lock you down in terms of path and action. Long-term *outcomes* are what you are trying to achieve over an extended period.

An organization needs to remain focused on long-term outcomes but can achieve them through multiple shorter-term strategies. OKRs should reflect, and seek to advance, the organization's purpose and its longer-term targets.

The board of directors also has a role to play here in ensuring focus on the long-term. First, the board should ensure that a leadership team is thinking about, and strategizing on, the future; that any strategies consider the long-term and are addressing long-term trends and forces. They should also ensure leadership is aligning activities and targets towards the organizational purpose and long-term targets. Board members should be engaged in creating long-term strategy to tap into areas of strategic expertise and knowledge.

Next, the board should require that leadership present annually how their work is achieving the organizational purpose and moving towards the long-term targets of the organization. This creates accountability and avoids the trap of short-termism. If an organization does not incorporate the organizational purpose and its long-term targets into shorter-term plans, then it might drift, miss targets, or fail to live up to its purpose. It might risk focusing only on short-term targets and could migrate away from activity that would see achievement of its purpose.

Therefore, to avoid the trap of short-termism, strategies and short-term plans need to demonstrate they reflect the organizational purpose, and reporting should be done yearly on the progress towards achieving that purpose and long-term targets.

Let's now explore the component pieces of an organizational strategy and its related plans.

Strategy and Plan Components

Given the shifting nature of strategies and plans, and the different approaches to the process, what necessary elements should an organization have in place? That's relatively straightforward and simple: a cascading structure starting with bigger-picture purpose and targets, working all the way down to an individual staff member's quarterly work plan (and then down to weekly and daily to-dos).

To be remarkable, an organization should have a cascading strategy and plan structure that creates a line of sight from today's activities to the purpose. You should have:

1. Organization purpose and North Star: your long-term objectives and target

2. Maximum three-year organization OKR: paints picture of where you want to be a few years out and what success looks like, and identifies major projects or investments planned for this horizon

3. Annual organization OKR: establishes objectives and success measures in a specific year; can be broken down quarterly if desired for tracking and monitoring

4. Annual department OKR: guides work of specific departments, and is built off, and rolls up to, organization OKR

5. Quarterly department OKR: allocates annual department OKRs by quarter and to specific staff; each KR has associated actions that outline the necessary approach to achieve the KR and that form the basis of allocation of work to team members

6. Individual quarterly work plans: establish the work program (and development goals) of each team member; are further broken down by the individual staff member into a weekly or daily "to-do list"

It might not look that way at first glance, but this structure is simple—there are only four elements of any level (objective, key result, action, and accountability). Several software solutions are available to digitize your OKR and facilitate the use of dashboards to monitor progress and performance.

With this kind of approach, you can see the key results over a multi-year timeline down to the daily to-do items of an individual staff member. It is critical that staff and teams at every level can understand and see how their work on a daily basis contributes to and aligns with where the organization aims to be in two to three years. I call this often-forgotten imperative the "line of sight."

Line of sight is an overlooked aspect of organizational success. Too many plans (and organizations, for that matter) don't achieve their potential because they fail to establish a line of sight between where an organization is going—the objective— and what someone is working on every day—the individual performance goals and projects. This creates focus drift and misaligned work efforts, and, at worst, disengagement from the purpose of the organization.

An effective approach regarding a line of sight is to consider the cascading nature of the series of strategies, OKRs and individual performance plans mentioned above. It looks like this:

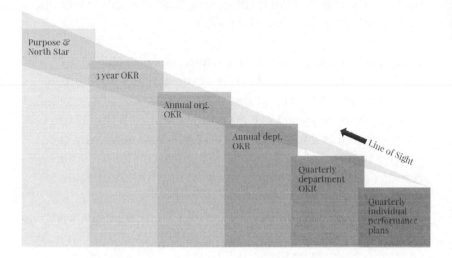

Viewing and building the strategies and plans in this format enables a line of sight that creates significant benefits for the organization and the team member:

- Team members, even the most junior, can see how the project they are working on rolls up to the purpose, North Star and multi-year strategy.

- Buy-in and support for the direction of the organization increases if people can see themselves in it and are making progress.

- Everyday work aligns visibly and experientially to the purpose of the organization.

Strategy drives an organization to look for new opportunities, anticipate and/or cause disruption and grow, versus continuing along a trajectory of the past. Strategies should be about advancement and the future, not repeating history. This is another important reason to have a strong and high-performing board of directors: so that they can advise and guide you on matters of the future, not the past.

In the end, the approach you use and the label that you give it are not necessarily important. It's crucial that you define a direction for the organization, and the measure of success that will tell you when you have arrived there. From there, you can empower teams and people to work towards achieving them. Progress and achievement can be measured against your key results or performance indicators. At any time, any team member should be able to know how the organization is progressing against multi-year, annual or quarterly objectives and targets, and their own role within that performance.

The Process to Build Strategy

Don't get sucked into doing a traditional strategy session as described at the opening of this chapter. If someone suggests that to you, run for the hills.

Getting to the right strategies or objectives requires strategic conversations, experiences and processes that are collaborative, creative, illustrative and disruptive. They should be infused with information and data, rich in ability to experience and gain insight, but they also need to push boundaries about what people think, believe or hold to be true. Building any strategy or plan should always challenge assumptions and beliefs, even the most foundational of them.

Expanding mindsets will be important to help get to new objectives. Share outside views, including those of past customers, or people who continually say no to your value proposition. Focus on information that is forward looking, that discusses how new models, customers and trends are affecting your organization, rather than on historical data and performance.

For an excellent resource for understanding how to construct engagement that will yield strategies and forward-looking objectives, see *Moments of Impact: How to Design Strategic Conversations that Accelerate Change* by Chris Ertel and Lisa Kay Solomon. In this book, the authors detail a five-step process to creating the space and approach for strategic discussions that help navigate complex and adaptive challenges. They identify useful strategies for getting beyond traditional thinking in strategy sessions and give examples of activities that can help people think in new and creative ways.

To the extent possible, be creative in the experiences in building your strategy. Find ways for the strategy team to experience insight and customer or member journeys. Find exercises and processes that enable them to think like their target market, and to think in ways that will push boundaries of traditional thinking. Rather than only relying on traditional brainstorming techniques, be open to finding ways that people can develop insight that can lead to even greater idea generation. Examples include workshops for creating a competing product, experiencing a product or service through their customer's seat, or writing the narrative of a finished product press release.

You may hire a consultant to lead this process, or you may do it internally. This may be a board-involved activity, or it may be staff only. You may make it for the leadership team only, or you may involve all staff. Regardless of the approach, ensure that the process, information and frame can deliver on the true nature of strategy as outlined in this chapter.

Key information to include in your strategy development process includes:

- Historical data on performance—of your organization, against peers or benchmarks, and against your purpose and long-term targets

- Trends and outlooks—affecting your sector, competitors, society, business, technology, and specifically your sector, including any exercises in foresight or future-casting. Here you may wish to test assumptions or traditionally held views

- Review of top performers, disruptive and emergent firms, and evolving business models—of peers, competitors and model organizations, including organizations that are not comparable to yours but have made significant change or impact

- Engagement—of your staff, board, customers, suppliers, contrarians, and past customers, ensuring good diversity of opinion and perspective.

- Views—what Ertel and Solomon call a "dream team" of people who hold prevalent views, cutting-edge views, contrarian views, user views, and adjacent possible views

The information and content are important. Equally important are the nature of the people and the discussions that happen so that you avoid repeating history and can look at new opportunities and objectives to be realized through a highly defined purpose and value proposition. OKRs should reflect progress towards the organization's purpose and long-term targets.

Finally, as will be discussed in the next chapter, you should also consider how digital and technology can be used to help transform your organization.

Here's a basic process to build your strategy, OKR, or an annual plan:

1. Identify who is to be on the working team. All staff? Leadership team? Team and board?

2. Identify and recruit internal and external people to be an engagement "dream team" who can provide you with a wide range of insight.

3. Collect the data, trend and outlook information outlined above, crunch the data, and make findings available to all participants in the process.

4. Hold a variety of strategic conversations with your engagement and working teams to test assumptions and views, and to help build understanding, shape choices or make decisions.

5. Using discussions, workshops, and other approaches, work through the information, trends and insights to generate potential objectives and key results for your organization to guide work and assess performance. This may be done for multiple years (a maximum of three) or an individual year. Refine, iterate and finalize. Assign accountabilities.

6. Break down the organizational objectives and key results into departmental OKRs to facilitate individual team members to develop their quarterly goals and plans.

7. Where necessary, seek final board approval, ensuring
    that the strategy reflects your organizational purpose
    and long-term key targets.

This is a generic approach, but it works. It creates a target and
measures of success. It breaks things down sufficiently that
people can align their work to the bigger purpose.

After you have your organizational or department OKR, the
leadership team should break down an annual plan into
manageable quarterly plans whereby actions or to-dos can be
generated for the quarterly key results. This facilitates the
allocation of work programs and goals for specific staff
members within different departments to ensure all
organizational targets will be achieved.

Performance Assessment and Measurement

A high-performance culture cannot be created unless
performance is rigorously tracked, measured, and reported.
Establishing metrics that are tracked and monitored is an
important way to ensure progress towards objectives, key
results and purpose. Regular reporting to leadership and board
provides accountability.

At the Calgary Chamber, we tracked and measured many key
results and indicators that showed how we were performing
against current year plan and our long-term targets. We would
measure ourselves against our peers through Association of
Chamber of Commerce Executives Dynamic Chamber
Benchmarking. In short, we did our best to ensure we were
moving in the right direction. A successful transformation and
Remarkability Agenda cannot take place unless you know

where you are going and are able to track progress in that direction.

Too many CEOs, including me, have fallen into the trap of wanting to be liked as opposed to holding people accountable. But in the end, a leader needs to ensure that the organization is delivering and performing, so a culture of performance measurement must be developed. This starts with the leader holding their team accountable for their targets, but also with the way that they themselves conduct meetings and discussions. These meetings and discussions should be focused on results and the necessary support needed to achieve those results. Holding people to account for their achievement, or lack thereof, is the only way to ensure that results will be achieved. The OKR approach supports accountability and performance measurement very well.

One of the beneficial features of the OKR approach and the simple means of identifying the performance measures is that the key results are quantitative and can be measured in terms of their progress and outcome. Performance against organizational, departmental and individual Key Results (KRs) should be tracked and monitored regularly, should be the focus of executive attention, and should be presented regularly to the board.

Some means of tracking real-time or current performance against KRs should be established. For the leadership team, this would be for the organizational OKRs and for the individual department leads this would be for their individual department OKRs. Progress to target KRs should be updated regularly to ensure that understanding of the situation takes place in as close to real time as possible. This can be done through some internal means such as a document or spreadsheet, or through existing OKR software platforms.

A regular meeting structure and approach, such as the one laid out in the matrix on the next page, can be used, among other things, as a regular means of tracking and accountability towards KRs progress:

MEETING TYPE	FOCUS	PARTIES INVOLVED
Quarterly Leadership Team Meeting	Assessment of completed quarter and achievement of organizational KRs Look forward to next quarter and associated KRs - Revision if necessary Strategic issue discussion	Leadership Team
Monthly Leadership Team Meeting	Check in on progress towards quarterly organizational KRs and discussion of any risks to achievement	Leadership Team
Monthly One-on-One Meeting	Check in on progress towards individual quarterly goals and departmental quarterly KRs	CEO and individual Leadership Team members Individual department leaders and their respective team members
Weekly Leadership Team Meeting	Quick dashboard review of progress towards organizational quarterly KRs Operational issues for this and following week	Leadership Team
Weekly Team Meetings	Check in on departmental progress/KRs	Individual department leaders and their team members

Creating a regular meeting cadence and a culture of performance assessment is critical for staff—but it must also be adopted by the board of directors. While the board may only need to meet 4-5 times per year, oversight of progress to plan and long-term targets is an essential element of the board's fiduciary role to ensure that the organization is achieving its targets and using its resources responsibly.

To ensure that the organizational leadership is performing, and to continue to keep the trust reservoir full, CEOs should report to the board every quarter on progress toward annual targets and should present at least annually on the progress towards long-term targets (e.g., the organizational purpose, North Star or the strategic plan key results). This ensures that you do not fall into the trap of short-termism and that you are demonstrably working towards the long-term. It is the leader's role to be focused on the long-term and by showing accountability and progress you will be able to show both board and stakeholders that your efforts are proving effective.

Resource Kit

Ask This—Diagnostic 6

(You can complete all diagnostic questions from each chapter online at www.makingremarkable.com)
Use a rating of Yes=1, No=0. A score of 80% or better indicates that you are likely remarkable in that element.

1. Multi-Year Strategy and Targets
    a. Does your organization have a clearly defined set of objectives and key results (i.e., does your organization know where it is going and when you will know it gets there, long and short-term performance targets, or a North Star)?
    b. Does your organization have a multi-year strategy developed within the last three years?
    c. Is your strategy no more than three years in horizon?

    d. Does your strategy enable flexibility, nimbleness and creativity in execution by not being overly prescriptive in terms of tactics and actions?

    e. Is there a line of sight created between this purpose, strategy, and individual staff quarterly plans (i.e., can staff appreciate how their daily work helps achieve long-term targets)?

2. Development of the Strategy

    a. Did you engage a broad cross section of stakeholders in developing your strategy?

    b. Is the strategy developed from the perspective of the customer/member?

    c. Did you evaluate trends, forces, competitors and opportunities in the development of your strategy?

    d. Did you question or challenge assumptions in the creation of your strategy?

    e. Did you assess the performance of the current business model in evaluating future options for the strategy?

3. Annual Plan and Targets

    a. Does your organization have an annual plan with objectives and key results tied to the longer-term purpose and strategy?

    b. Do you present progress towards the long-term targets at least annually to the board?

    c. Is the annual plan performance tracked and reviewed at least quarterly, with results presented to board and staff?

    d. Do you have adequate meeting structures and approaches in place to ensure oversight of performance and accountability of the organization to its targets?

e. Is your strategy and associated key results known by all staff?

Do This to be Remarkable

- Set targets.
  - Be clear about where the organization is going. Establish a North Star that is the ultimate metric of how your customers realize value from you. Make it bold and inspiring.
  - Establish achievable but stretch targets on the way there.

- Go lightweight.
  - Use an OKR approach to strategy and planning to enable flexibility, accountability and performance.
  - Follow a process that uses broad base information and insight and engages the right people in strategic discussions to help formulate the directions for the organization.
  - Challenge deeply-held beliefs and assumptions. Build the future, not a repeat of the past.

- Stay nimble and flexible.
  - An OKR approach means you can be flexible and responsive to changes in the world around you, or to opportunities that arise.
  - Continuous research, investigation and inquiry will help team members to stay on top of current trend and disruptions. Nothing in a plan or strategy should remain if it is being trumped by something newly emerging or more pressing. Being willing to change mid-stream is important.
  - Remain nimble and flexible but focus on the long-term. Never neglect the purpose or North Star, and report regularly on the progress

towards long-term targets so that the organization does not drift.

- Integrate and connect.
  - o Strategies and plans should be integrative and interconnected across departments, with clear accountabilities. So much of what happens in the modern organization is not siloed and needs cross-departmental collaboration and support.

- Create a line of sight.
  - o Create line of sight for the whole organization between purpose and North Star, long-term OKR and individual quarterly goals so that everyone knows where you are heading, what the targets are, and how their own work fits into the bigger picture.

- Review, regularly.
  - o This goes for progress against targets, but also for relevance of specific strategies. Quarterly reviews at the organizational and individual level can be used to examine the progress toward targets.
  - o Track and measure performance, regularly and richly. Always know where you are according to plan and target. Use good and current data. Report to leadership and board on progress to maintain trust and confidence, and to seek support and guidance where necessary.

Review This

- BOOKS
  - o Andrew Grove, *High Output Management.* Vintage (1995).
  - o Chris Ertel and Lisa Kay Salomon, *Moments of Impact: How to Design Strategic Conversations*

That Accelerate Change. Simon & Schuster (2014).

o Salim Ismail, *Exponential Organizations: Why new organizations are ten times better, faster, and cheaper than yours (and what to do about it)*. Diversion Books (2014).

o Renee Mauborgne and W. Chan Kim, *Blue Ocean Strategy: How to Create Uncontested Market Space and Make the Competition Irrelevant*. Harvard Business Review Press (2005).

o Rita Gunther McGrath, *The End of Competitive Advantage*: *How to Keep Your Strategy Moving As Fast As Your Business*. Harvard Business Review Press (2013).

o Jeremy Gutsche, *Better and Faster: The Proven Path to Unstoppable Ideas*. Crown Business (2015).

o Peter Thiel, *Zero to One: Notes on Startups, or How to Build the Future*. Crown Business (2014).

o Lawrence Freedman, *Strategy: A History*. Oxford University Press (2013).

- OTHER
  o David Collis and Michael Rukstad, "Can You Say What Your Strategy Is?" *Harvard Business Review*, April 2008. https://hbr.org/2008/04/can-you-say-what-your-strategy-is

  o Roger L. Martin, "The Big Lie of Strategic Planning." *Harvard Business Review*, January-February 2014. https://hbr.org/2014/01/the-big-lie-of-strategic-planning

  o How Google Ventures sets up OKR https://www.youtube.com/watch?v=mJB83EZtAjc

CHAPTER 11: Platform: Digital and Technology

What is it?	Digital and technology is the ability to support and amplify your value proposition by applying new technology solutions to the way in which you do business, understand and interact with your target market, and provide value and benefit to members.
Why is it important?	Ability to gain better data and intelligence, more rapidly deploy value, make life easier for customer and staff, generate savings.
Where do you start?	• Find the right talent. • Build a digital strategy. • Allocate sufficient resources to implement.
Remarkable is:	• An organization that has embraced digital and data as part of its culture and DNA • An organization with a strong digital strategy, and has secured the leadership and resources to implement • Processes, procedures and activities that have been digitized • Data that is captured and turned into knowledge • A value proposition and business model that are enabled and augmented by digital technologies

"Just because digital technology makes connecting possible doesn't mean that you're actually reaching people." Maureen Dowd[20]

Ask any chamber of commerce or association what one of their biggest annoyances is and you'll inevitably hear "Events"— specifically, the logistics around events. While events generate good revenue, the reality is that they are an intense pain in the arse in terms of logistics and staff time.

Setting up the event on your website or registration system. Chasing down the names of the people at tables purchased by a member. Allocating individual tickets to unfilled tables in the room. Using a spreadsheet and hand-drawn picture to figure out where to put each table in the room based on member status. Printing name tags and stuffing name badges. Printing multiple copies of the registration list, sorted by name, by company, by table number. Laying out name badges at the event. Printing new name badges on site if names are spelled incorrectly. Sifting through pages of registrants for the inevitable person who "is sure" they registered but didn't, or the guest who can't remember who invited them or even what company they were invited by. It's a gong show. It's almost not worth it.

Now, imagine if you could fix all that.

Imagine a system that lets the purchaser register all the names of their table guests themselves, without any involvement of your staff. That automatically allocates individual ticket purchasers to unfilled tables. That lets you move tables throughout the room using a virtual floorplan, "dragging and dropping" tables or individuals into different locations. An email automatically reminds people of the event, location, and their table number. Staff shows up on site with a few iPads, digitally checking in each registrant. The digital check-in sends a command to print a name tag on demand. The guest walks a few paces to the next table and is greeted by name and handed their just-printed name tag, including table number and company. If the guest is a VIP or prospect, a text notification will have been sent to a staff member, who will greet the guest and bring them to their table or facilitate meaningful introductions. You end the event with a digital record of attendees, their contact details. . . and satisfied customers. It all seems so effortless and enjoyable. *Now* it seems worth it. This is the power of technology and it's how the Calgary Chamber now manages its events.

That's just a small snapshot of what digital technologies can do for an organization. It's not the furthest reaches of the digital universe, but it represents exactly what enhanced digital capability should do for an organization: reduce stress and demand on staff time, facilitate the delivery of the value proposition, increase the effortlessness of the guest experience, enable data capture and analytics, build knowledge, enhance decision making, and ultimately increase profitability. Remarkable organizations are increasingly digital organizations.

The Imperative to Go Digital

Digital transformation should be near the top of every leader's agenda. If it isn't, you are at risk of becoming irrelevant. If you're spending more time debating the issue of a golf tournament or gala than you are discussing how to better integrate digital capabilities and technologies, consider that a warning sign. If you aren't discussing the future of your organization from a digital perspective, you should be.

Many organizations like chambers and member-based associations have seen their value proposition eroded because of technologies like LinkedIn (networking), Twitter (news and information dissemination), and TED or YouTube (events). When those things came along, few organizations saw them as competitive threats. They were all too slow to react, and they lost both efficacy and members.

Now, consider the fact that those technologies are the tip of the iceberg. Right now, a host of innovators are trying to put organizations like yours out of business. It's happening everywhere. Look at banking, transportation, and retail—all traditional industries dying on the vine. If you think a member-based organization is immune, then you need a reset. Your future is at risk.

As a CEO charged with transformation, you want to be making *digital* transformation a fundamental part of your overall transformation. It must be part of the DNA.

Digital transformation doesn't just mean getting a website or joining social media, although those are parts of it. It is not your IT department or helpdesk. It is not deciding which software to use. A digital transformation includes those things but is much larger. It is the use of digital technologies to advance and enable the value proposition in new and better ways. Your digital transformation will encompass the overall system and platforms, as well as staff engagement and adoption of the technologies. It will become the DNA of your organization.

At the Calgary Chamber, I took the digital imperative so seriously that I created a whole new Digital and Technology department, added a senior director to the Leadership Team, and gave him the mandate to develop and implement a digital strategy that would reach across and within the organization. His objective was to make the Calgary Chamber the most digitally advanced chamber in the world. He was given resources to test, iterate, build, and innovate within the organization.

Within the first eighteen months, he had:

1. Developed a proprietary online diagnostic engine

2. Developed a Chamber University for training staff and new hires on our technology platform

3. Produced a digital election and campaign platform that enabled our chamber to engage with candidates, and for members to send pre-populated advocacy letters to elected officials

4. Transformed the event experience (see the description at the beginning of this chapter)

5. Brought the entire organization onto MS Teams for collaboration and engagement

6. Explored facial recognition software for event registration and mapping of people's digital networks for business development and matchmaking purposes

7. Completed other cool, remarkable and highly top-secret stuff

I viewed our digital focus as our own "X[21]", or skunkworks, department. We didn't have as many expectations on this investment, and relaxed some of the rules around ROI, time and outcome—simply because we needed a way to enable an unproven and untested idea to spend enough time in development that we could see if it would work. I encourage all leaders to find that thing they are willing to suspend judgement and traditional metrics on as their "moonshot" or "X" department.

Time will tell if the Calgary Chamber achieves all that it can digitally, but for now, I am confident it is at the leading edge of global chambers in its use of digital technologies and the move to digital transformation. And we are in good company. Both the Dubai Chamber of Commerce and Industry and the New South Wales (Australia) Business Chamber have made considerable investments and movement into the digital realm.

They both view the application and integration of digital from the same standpoint as me—capture and mine robust data to deploy a more custom and targeted value proposition that delivers more without having to show up, all while making life easier for staff and members.

What Does Going Digital Look Like?

There are different stages and degrees of going digital:

1. Digital: typically, a broad term used to encompass the online presence, including a website and social media.

2. Digitization: the application of digital products to enable better operational performance of your organization. It includes use of the cloud, and new platforms to help deliver your product and services such as online event registration or membership renewal.

3. Digital transformation: the modification of the business model and enhancement of the value proposition through digital means so that you can begin to offer new value. It requires the capture and use of data to increase knowledge and includes the application of new technology to the business model canvas (as explored in Chapter 9).

Many organizations have stepped into the digital and digitization realm. Most however have not fully digitized, nor have they moved to digital transformation. Your goal ultimately should be digital transformation, but you need to walk before you can run.

An organization like a chamber of commerce is there to help its members be more successful businesses. As discussed in Chapter 9, doing this requires deep knowledge of your members, particularly their largest problems or pain points, so that you can deliver a product, service or experience that addresses that pain point. Digital transformation is ultimately about using technology to know your members so well through their actions, interests, and preferences that you can deliver new and innovative value to them without them having to ask for it. That, in a nutshell, is digital transformation.

Let's break that down. Customers and members want value, they want exceptional, effortless experiences, and they don't always want to have to show up to get it. Digital transformation enables the delivery of value and the creation of effortless experiences. It enables an organization to create targeted value to audience segments by capturing and analyzing sufficient amounts of data that indicate the business problems customers face, or the kind of company they want to do business with. That data is turned into knowledge to be used in the creation of new value.

The organization can create curated and even customized value in terms of events, connections to future customers, information and data, or advocacy. This is all done using data analytics captured based on what the member tells about themselves and their past behaviour in terms of events, articles and information read or viewed and other forms of engagement. The customer or member will never need to ask, "What is going on at the chamber?" or should never be able to say, "I didn't see value in my membership or donation."

Imagine a time when, based on the accurate data that an organization has about a customer or member, that customer receives a "mass customized" weekly e-newsletter that includes

only topics, issues and events that they are interested in.
Imagine if that same newsletter also has targeted ads specific to
their interests or company focus. Imagine an executive sitting
at their desk and getting an email that proactively updates them
on progress of a business or policy issue they are following.
Imagine a member getting a notification that they should
connect with another business because an algorithm has found
that the chances of them doing business together is over 80%.

Imagine a sales or fund development team that can distribute
sales packages customized to a prospect, be informed when that
package is reviewed, generate an invoice once agreement has
been reached, and automatically issue a social media post when
that new customer pays their invoice—seamlessly integrated.
Imagine a member walking into a ballroom for an event and
having facial recognition immediately check them in and print
off their name badge.

Imagine how satisfied customers and members would be if this
was their experience. That is value for them and ROI. All of
this, and more, is possible with digital transformation and
investment. By the time I left the Calgary Chamber at the end of
2017, we had done some, though not all, of this. This set of
examples represents the scale of thinking and approach that the
chamber aims to achieve.

A digital organization is a data-driven organization. No more
decisions based on gut or feel. Its "digital and data first" mantra
ensures that people are looking to optimize the business
operation and its delivery of the value proposition through a
digital lens. That value creation is performed through capturing
and analyzing good data. Therefore, processes and culture are
established to be continually looking to capture data.

Organizations like chambers and other member-based organizations should be shifting their mindsets to increasingly being digital and data organizations. Building an organization to be successful in the future will require (re)engineering it around the data capture and analysis functions; digital transformation will deliver value based on the knowledge and insight it creates. Additionally, the selling of data could generate a revenue stream, as so few accurate business information databases exist. Imagine the power and value of robust data about the needs, preferences and actions of businesses or members.

Over time, the data will also enable real-time evaluation of value propositions to ensure that they are meeting the needs of customers and members, as known from the data. If done correctly, there should be no excuse for an organization to have an outdated value proposition. It should be assessed and adjusted in real time as the data on customers or members demonstrates needs, preferences and wants.

Realities of Digital

It is not easy to transform digitally. Websites and social media are important but are just early steps along that journey. Here are a few realities of a digital transformation:

- Companies and platforms like Google, Uber, and Amazon can engage with millions of people across wide geographic territories. The reach and scale of your organization will be vastly smaller. Therefore, the scale that is expected or touted in the traditional digital realm can be difficult to achieve for organizations like chambers or associations.

- ROI is hard to establish. Prior to any implementation, ROI will be tough to quantify as you will have no data. Try to find ways to quantify ROI in the case for transformation. For example, if doing name tags for events takes staff 2 hours every event, multiplied by 40 events a year, you can make the case for on-demand name tag printing by showing the productivity regained by the team.

- Digital transformation does have risk—including cost—and many smaller organizations are risk averse because they cannot afford to let a project fail. Nothing you do however should risk the farm but heading down the digital transformation path means you will need to find a way to become more comfortable with the risk associated with digital.

- From my experience, the equation of digital transformation is that the tool, software or platform is 25% of the equation, and adoption and usage is 75%. The organization must be fully committed to digital adoption for the investment to be successful. This means you need to support the change with effective case building, education, implementation, and ongoing support. Organizational buy-in is essential.

There will need to be a cultural shift to support more digital. The team will need to be more open to change and adopting new ways of working. People will need to think about delivering value through the digital platform. Data capture will need to be a priority and people will need to be trained in how to analyze that data to find opportunities to deliver new value. Change management and a cultural shift in the importance of digital and data are essential to success.

The Benefits of Going Digital

The benefits of going digital should be self-evident. They include:

- Increased value in the eyes of customers and members, hence greater revenues

- Greater potential reach due to increased delivery of value without having to be present or actively involved

- Greater relevance to younger demographics (aka your future members) who are more tech-savvy and less interested in having to show up to receive value

- Reduced staffing costs through the digitization of many functions and traditionally labour-intensive work

- Not fast tracking your organization into irrelevance

Moving to Digital

Don't waste time debating the move to digital—it's an existential necessity for most organizations. Focus on talking about how quickly, how much to allocate to it and who is to lead it.

If organizational "will" is behind a digital transformation, the move has four key ingredients.

Hire or Promote a Strong Digital Lead

This is someone who understands digital technologies and platforms, particularly digital big picture, policies and the integrating systems to create sound data structures that can be mined and analyzed for value. Few organizations have this kind of skill set on staff. Invest in a specialist; it will be a solid use of your resources.

This role should be given an elevated status in the organization, ideally sitting on the leadership team and reporting to the CEO. It is a strategic role and should be protected from such day-to-day requirements as deskside IT support. Your digital lead will never get things done if people are constantly asking them why their screen went blank.

In this role, you will need someone who is technically capable and experienced in digital. You may be tempted to promote a digital marketer, or the person responsible for your social media. Resist this urge. The scope and scale of this role goes well beyond the use of social media and requires technical knowledge of systems, platforms and technologies.

Your digital lead should actively network with their peers in other organizations to share and learn. Things are happening so quickly that peer learning and sharing will help to accelerate digital transformation. Additionally, by sharing and collaborating on studies, research and even implementations, organizations can stretch resources farther than if trying to do it all themselves. For example, a group of digital leads from a handful of organizations could get together to fund a study evaluating the most advanced association or chamber CRM systems that will meet their digital transformation needs.

Ideally, your board will have someone experienced in digital and technology to provide guidance from a strategic perspective. This will help to ensure conversations at a strategic level are supported by a "believer" who can help make the argument for investments and actions in this domain. If your board does not have this skill set or capability, consider adding it to the current requirements list for recruitment.

Develop a Digital Strategy

Every organization will have different needs in terms of digital transformation tools and investments, so it is outside the scope of *Making Remarkable* to recommend specific solutions. Organizations must develop a digital strategy that is right for their own digital vision, resource base, capabilities, existing technologies and value proposition.

A digital strategy should include what the move to digital will entail and what steps and accountabilities need to be in place to ensure success. At the Calgary Chamber, our goal was to become the global chamber that knows its members the best; we would achieve that through digital transformation and the way it would support staff performance, data capture, productivity and value proposition delivery.

The digital strategy should have a future-focused orientation— it should consider where the technology, organization, target market and customer needs are going, rather than looking at current needs and offerings. The digital strategy needs to skate where the puck is going.

The digital strategy at the Calgary Chamber reflected such goals as creating integrated digital systems for data capture and analysis, developing a culture of digital-first, building a suite of tools that enable better data-driven decisions, improving productivity, evolving the digital offering for members, and exploring new revenue streams from new tools and applications.

Allocate Resources

With a digital lead in place, an organization will need to begin implementing its digital strategy. That will take resources— specifically, money, so the digital strategy should include a high-level budget, to be overseen by the lead, who should be seeking board approval for access to those funds.

While some of the strategy can be implemented using existing resources, building a viable digital organization will require you to spend money on things like software and consultants. Don't labour under any notion that this can be done on the cheap. Not everyone needs to get the Mercedes version, but many implementations will take thousands, if not tens of thousands, of dollars. The ROI, over time, should be well worth the investment. Your board and team should be made aware that there is in fact a greater risk of not acting than in taking the risk to do something.

Where will organizations find the money? Strategic reserves or rainy-day funds are ideal places to look; what could be more strategic or better deployed to avoid a rainy day than digital investments?

Some organizations may consider raising revenues through a small fee increase or may look to set a specific "digital levy" on top of stable fees. Re-allocation of revenues from some other aspects of the business may also make sense. Other organizations may be lucky in finding a sponsor willing to support a digital transformation. However, the funds are raised, sourcing them to support the implementation of a digital strategy is essential.

Reinforce Internally

We can all think back to new technologies or software that promised to make life easier and reduce worktime by 20%. Or the one new piece of hardware that would replace three others. I bet that most of you aren't working more efficiently, and that you are still using all three pieces of hardware. And paper for that matter.

In my career, I have overseen or been part of five CRM implementations. Each one promised newer and better features. Each one touted that one element that would make our jobs perfect. And each one of them were major disappointments. Why? Because without the right internal reinforcement, a new technology will be no better than the old technology, and because humans hate change. They'll stick with what they know.

The digital lead will need to be very strategic about digital transformation. The role will be as much about change management as digital. They will be bringing in new ways of work, new tools and new requirements, all which will create upheaval in the organization.

First, the lead must develop the policies, procedures and approaches that people will need to follow to make the transformation successful. Switching CRMs to capture new data? Well, make it clear what data needs to be captured and why that is essential. Rolling out new digital event software? Make it clear that people can no longer handwrite names on the guest list.

Any digital transformation requires internal support, adoption and integration. First, the digital lead should talk to people about the rationale and the need for digital transformation. Following the Remarkability Agenda design format from

Chapter 4 is a sound approach; it will paint the picture, show why it will be better, and enable people to see themselves reflected in the change.

The next step is leadership endorsement. The CEO and the whole leadership team must evangelize this investment and change: speak positively about it, use it, and reinforce its importance with the team.

Once you have buy in, rollout is next. The digital lead must craft a thoughtful and detailed roll out plan that gives people ample insight into the change, when it will happen, and how it will happen. Training and deskside support may be necessary in early stages and having a power user or internal champion on the team is vital so that peers know where to turn for answers or help. Ongoing check-ins on how the rollout has gone are essential, as are regular updates and walk-arounds to make sure people are using the new tools.

Nothing is worse than when a new piece of software is rolled out by flicking a switch, with no user help or support. I have seen a rollout in which an email was sent to potential users with little more than a link to the software's YouTube promo video. As you can imagine, that was a rollout that didn't stick all that well.

After rollout, move to reinforcing the culture of digital and data. Leaders and heavy users will need to be vocal about how and why to use the new approach. Benefits and ROI will need to be shown. Reinforcement at every step will be critical, so that people continue to support the digital transformation.

Resource Kit

Ask This—Diagnostic 7

(You can complete all diagnostic questions from each chapter online at www.makingremarkable.com)
Use a rating of Yes=1, No=0. A score of 80% or better indicates that you are likely remarkable in that element.

1. Strategy and Mindset
   a. Do you have a digital strategy—beyond your website, social media and base IT—encompassing the entire organization and operation?
   b. Does your organization reflect a "digital first" mindset in terms of activities, functions, delivery of value and business model?
   c. Is your organization always looking at new ways to deploy the value proposition via digital means?
   d. Does your organization value data as a strategic asset to use to grow the business?
   e. Do you use and analyze data you capture to support decisions, create intelligence, and to improve the value proposition or member experience?

2. Time and Resources
   a. Is there a digital lead or department responsible for digital and technology, and the implementation of the digital strategy?
   b. Does your digital lead have a senior strategic role at the leadership table, and is this person tasked with organization wide strategy development and execution?

c. Do you spend more time as a team or board talking about digital than you do events and golf tournaments?

d. Does your organization have money set aside or earmarked for digital investments or implementation of your digital strategy?

e. Do you have digital policies and procedures that support the adoption of digital transformation in your organization?

Do This to be Remarkable

- Free your mind.
  - Leaders must believe in the power and potential of digital technologies to be a critical part of their organization's future. This is not about a website or social media; this is how digital and technology enables the value proposition by making you more current, relevant, proactive, nimble and targeted.
  - Think big and bold, don't dismiss or be afraid of some of the ideas that come forward. The day before every innovation becomes mainstream, it was a crazy idea.

- Find someone to lead the digital transformation and chart the path.
  - You will need a technically capable person experienced in digital to be your lead on this.
  - Task this person with coordinating and overseeing the creation and implementation of a digital strategy.

- Dig deep into your pockets.
  - You will need to allocate sufficient resources to make digital transformation happen. It cannot be done on a shoestring, and additional monies

will need to be diverted or re-allocated to achieve a truly digital organization.

- Make it stick.
  - Embed and reinforce a digital- and data-first approach within the organization through change management, positive support, cultural adoptions and demonstration of value and benefit.
  - Break some rules or suspend some traditional metrics to give digital a decent enough chance to be successful, as this is new territory that won't likely perform similar to other investments. It needs some time and nurturing free from the normal rules.

Review This

- OTHER
  - Gerald T.Kane, "Don't Forget the Basics in Digital Transformation" *MIT Sloan Management Review* https://sloanreview.mit.edu/article/dont-forget-the-basics-in-digital-transformation/
  - Janet Hughes, "What a Digital Organization Looks Like" *Medium* https://medium.com/doteveryone/what-a-digital-organisation-looks-like-82426a210ab8
  - Jacques Bughin et. al., "Why digital strategies fail" *McKinsey and Co. Quarterly Review* https://www.mckinsey.com/business-functions/digital-mckinsey/our-insights/why-digital-strategies-fail?cid=other-eml-alt-mkq-mck-oth-1803&hlkid=00aea097823f4b59a4b6107b75df0dc6&hctky=10297945&hdpid=e2983bdc-4cc8-4069-9cb7-948cdddd5004

CHAPTER 12: Platform: Finances (A Deeper Dive)

What is it?	Your financial situation will determine your ability to stay alive, and to undertake your Remarkability Agenda.
Why is it important?	Money and profit create sustainability and an opportunity to become, and remain, remarkable by investing in the organization, people and the value proposition.
Where do you start?	• Assess the financial health of the organization. • Make any changes needed to grow revenue and reduce expenses.
Remarkable is:	• A profitable organization that has sufficient cash to cover its obligations. • Streamlined expense profile. • Maximized revenue performance. • An organization that is stable or improving in its positive financial performance. • Has financial reserves to pay for strategic and transformational projects.

"Show me the money." Rod Tidwell from Jerry Maguire[22]

One of the biggest challenges that a CEO often faces is a poor (if not bleak) financial situation, usually the result of previous poor management and leadership, an inability to deliver a solid value proposition, and not understanding how to effectively manage the finances of an operation.

Your Remarkability Agenda will require funds. But in most instances, these funds are not readily available or are inadequate to do everything you want or need to do. This means that you must:

1. Assess the current financial picture.
2. Execute opportunities for expense reduction and revenue increases.
3. Prioritize the desired investments and projects that are part of your Remarkability Agenda and identify how you will secure the needed resources.

Before we delve into the financial piece, it is important to stress one point: fixing an organization's financial situation is usually not about fixing the finances; it's about delivering value. Customers and members will pay for something if they feel it has value. Too many transformation efforts are driven by the finances and evaluated by the finances. The finances are in fact an outcome, not an action.

The goal should be to address the underlying deficiency in the value proposition. Whether that is through a clearer purpose, providing better programs, delivering greater advocacy, offering new events or experiences, expanding choice and digital capability, making options more accessible or by helping create better connections, delivering a better value proposition will help create better financial performance. As the board chair who hired me said: "You can't cut your way to greatness." Don't get sucked into the expense-slashing-as-solution trap. Work effectively with your board, finance committee and colleagues to ensure that's the perspective brought forward in your work.

This chapter will cover:

1. Financial analyses that can be done to understand the health of the organization's finances.
2. Ways to cut expenses and drive revenue.
3. Ideas to prioritize and pay for transformation.

Financial Analyses

Getting a firm picture of the finances is critical. Recall that, at a minimum, the following analyses are recommended:

1. Organizational profitability, current and historical, and departmentally/functionally if possible

2. Productivity of revenue-generating resources such as sales and sponsorship, determining the net income of all the sales revenues brought in versus their cost/expense to the organization

3. Retention and conversion rates; how many customers/members repeat business, and how long does it take to get a sale?

4. Historical cash balance and annual cycles

5. Balance of investments/restricted funds and historical returns and balances

6. Revenue and expense historical growth rates and cyclicality

7. Staff expense percentage of total expenses, and growth in salary expense over time

8. Net income and margin of revenue areas (i.e., events, conferences)

9. Historical average sale value and per customer expenditures annually

These analyses will give you a sense of the historical and current finances of the organization. It will show you trends to assess how it is performing now versus periods in the past. It will give you a sense of what is producing returns for you and what is not even covering costs. Finally, it will give insight into the movements and patterns of your customers/members in terms of their retention, adoption and willingness to pay over time. All of this can be used to paint a picture of where there is strength and where there is weakness in the financial outcomes of the organization.

Expense Reductions

The temptation is always to cut expenses to deliver a target budget. Whether that is cutting people, space or coffee, it is usually the first place that a new CEO can head to. It can be effective, if there truly is excess to be trimmed. But it is often not the most effective action, for it can lead to further challenges down the road.

Assuming that the financial analyses identify opportunities to reduce expenses, here are some considerations:

1. Do you have too many staff? Can you reduce your headcount?

2. Are revenue-generating resources creating a return for the organization? Can they be better deployed?

3. Can you cut certain activities or events that do not generate a positive return for the organization, thereby saving money?

4. Can you cut expenses or renegotiate contracts to improve event and function margins?

5. Is there room to reduce your real estate costs?

6. Are there any service provider expenses that can be renegotiated or reduced for things such as copiers, coffee, cleaning, office supplies, telecommunications, IT, HR, or legal?

7. Do you really need all that stationery?

8. Can you cut expenses such as office cleaning and copier servicing by reducing their frequency, without affecting productivity?

9. Do you really need all the service provider contracts that you currently have?

10. Do you need to provide food at every meeting you host, or can people get by on just coffee?

11. Are you paying for a Mercedes when a Toyota will do?

These and other ways of looking to trim costs can help to give you a sound financial foundation upon which to build a transformation. However, there are certain areas that you should be mindful of not cutting too drastically or eliminating:

1. Professional development and learning for staff

2. Reserve fund contributions

3. Digital and IT investments (the importance of which was discussed in Chapter 11; clearly define IT expenses versus investments)

4. Critical staff functions

Revenue Growth

As mentioned earlier, it is difficult to cut your way to greatness. Often it is about driving more and better revenue, not reducing expenses. The roots of better revenue lie in a better value proposition, but other elements of your revenue profile might bring about some quick wins:

1. How long has it been since you raised your prices? Is this a possibility?

2. Do you have underpaying customers/members who might be brought to a more reasonable level?

3. Do you have any assets that you can sell or monetize? This could be as big as a building, as small as a magazine, or as impactful as a piece of software.

4. Is there appetite among your members for a "transformation" surcharge on their next invoice to help fund the transformation?

5. Can you seek funding from any foundations or programs?

6. Are there any assets that are sponsorable that are not currently sponsored? Would any customer or member sponsor parts of the transformation (either in cash or in kind)?

7. Are there opportunities to sell advertising?

8. Are there passive income streams you can create because of your customer base?

9. Are there opportunities for you to be a contract service provider to other organizations in your community, for events or back office functions like accounting?

These are some basic questions to get your revenue ideas percolating. Regardless of the opportunities to grow revenue, ultimately it is the value proposition that needs to be addressed to create long-term and more sustainable revenue growth and stability. Addressing the value proposition was tackled in Chapter 9.

Paying for Transformation

As you have seen throughout this book, a Remarkability Agenda will generate many places to spend money. That is inevitable. Many organizations simply will not have the funds to pay for all the ideas set forth here, let alone all of them at once. Therefore, prioritization and planning will be required to pay for what is needed.

The first step will be to review what is needed under your Remarkability Agenda and determine priorities. Of all the potential projects discussed in this book—rebranding, values exercise, digital investments, governance review or board survey, HR support, value proposition analysis—a CEO will need to prioritize those that make the most sense for the specific organization.

Once a prioritized list of projects has been created and agreed to by the board, including a realistic schedule for getting them completed, the next step is to secure the resources for each project. Some ideas for funds include:

1. Rainy day or reserve/restricted funds

2. Strategic investment fund

3. Sponsors or patrons (providing cash or in-kind)

4. Space created by expense reductions/revenue growth

5. Future year budgets (budgeted in for future years as a strategic expense)

6. Diversion of funds from a previously planned expense to a transformational expense

7. Deficit budget

Each organization will prioritize different investments in the Remarkability Agenda and will pay for them differently. There is no right answer here but ensuring that funds are available to undertake this work is a requirement, for it cannot all be done internally.

Small Budget, Maximum Impact

I recognize that my experiences and the approach that I have taken at the Calgary Chamber are from a privileged place of an organization that is relatively large and has considerable financial capability. Most organizations are not like that. In fact, most of the thousands of chambers or associations across

North America are small shops with perhaps two or three employees and an annual budget of a few hundred thousand dollars. Many times, they ask me: with our limited budget, what's the best bang for the buck?

The answer to that question is: it depends. It depends on what the customer or member base in any given community values the most or believes creates the greatest ROI. Understanding your customer (see Chapter 9) will help you develop a sense of what will be most valued. At the end of the day, the most important things to spend your limited resources on are the things that will deliver value and ROI to your customer.

Based on what I have experienced, and in discussions with other chamber leaders, the areas of expense that generally seem to offer the best return are:

- Programs that help them grow their business – such as new markets and new business lines/revenue streams

- High-quality (which is not the same as high-frequency) event experiences with great speakers

- Networking opportunities that create real and meaningful connections for members

- Digital presence: a high-quality and well-designed website, social media and web-based capability for members (i.e., event registration, bill payment, networking and interactions, etc.)

- High-quality and performing sales people

Resource Kit

Ask This—Diagnostic 8

(You can complete all diagnostic questions from each chapter online at www.makingremarkable.com)
Use a rating of Yes=1, No=0. A score of 80% or better indicates that you are likely remarkable in that element.

1. Financial Metrics
    a. Do you undertake regular (i.e., at least annual) financial analyses that show current performance against historical performance to identify trends?
    b. Do you have acceptable retention rates, better than 80% and in line with peers?
    c. Are your sales assets productive (i.e., are sales, retention, sponsorship and business development people bringing in more – target 2-3x – what they are costing you)?
    d. Are your expense ratios and levels in line with your peer group (excluding technology, which is typically underfunded)?
    e. Have your financial metrics been improving over the past three years?

2. Financial Position
    a. Is your organization profitable?
    b. Do you have sufficient cash balances throughout the year and are you capable of covering all financial obligations?
    c. Have you decreased your expenses to the lowest level possible?
    d. Have you found and mobilized all possible revenue streams?

e. Do you have enough money to help make your organization remarkable, such as through investment in brand, people, and digital and technology?

Do This to be Remarkable

- Assess the financial health of the organization.
  - ○ Conduct a range of financial analyses to get a picture of the organization's financial performance and health as a means of guiding the transformation and discerning your ability to pay for it.

- Deliver financial performance.
  - ○ Be profitable.
  - ○ Have sufficient cash balance.
  - ○ Ensure assets (e.g., sales and business development) are financially productive.
  - ○ Have a sufficient reserve fund to enable strategic or transformation projects. You should be able to annually spend between 3-5% of revenues on strategic projects from your strategic reserve fund.

- Make necessary changes and decisions to get on track.
  - ○ If the financial picture of the organization is not where you want it to be, make the necessary expense reductions, revenue increases and shifts in value proposition to make it happen.

- Figure out how to pay for transformation and remarkability.
  - ○ The pathway to remarkability will cost money. Assess options within your organization to pay for the necessary change and transformation.

Review This

- BOOKS
    - Harrison Coerver and Mary Byers, CAE, *Race for Relevance: 5 Radical Changes for Associations*. ASAE The Centre for Association Leadership (2011).
    - Harrison Coerver and Mary Byers, CAE, *Road to Relevance: 5 Strategies for Competitive Associations*. ASAE The Centre for Association Leadership (2013).

- OTHER
    - National Association of Corporate Directors website and materials: www.nacdonline.org
    - Institute of Corporate Directors website and materials: https://www.icd.ca/Resource-Centre.aspx
    - Chartered Professional Accountants reports: https://www.cpacanada.ca/en/business-and-accounting-resources/strategy-risk-and-governance or www.aicpa.org
    - American Society of Association Executives materials: www.asaecenter.org
    - Canadian Society of Association Executives materials: www.csae.com

CHAPTER 13: Staying Remarkable

Achieving remarkability is a lot like losing weight - you have worked your arse off to get there and now you don't want to do anything to slip back. But it can be easy and tempting to be complacent or a little less disciplined. That's when it all starts to slide away.

Many organizations are fighting for their lives because they either didn't see the change coming that has so significantly impacted their success, didn't respond to the change, didn't believe it would affect them, or simply paused to bask in their own awesomeness. The reality is that leaders need to always be adapting their organizations.

Jeremy Gutsche, CEO of TrendHunter and author of *Better and Faster: The Proven Path to Unstoppable Ideas,* suggests that leaders need to cultivate a hunter approach rather than a farmer approach. Gutsche describes the hunter as insatiable, curious, willing to destroy and never complacent. Complacency of performance, of position, is the death knell of so many organizations—as many of us are all too aware. Being remarkable means being, valuing and hiring people who are hunters.

As discussed previously in *Making Remarkable*, achieving remarkability is not something that has an end state. There is no "done." You cannot set and forget, and you cannot ever take your eye off the prize. Once you decide to become remarkable, staying remarkable is a practice of diligence, discipline and vigilance.

The good news is that if you are well into, or have completed, your Remarkability Agenda, much of what you have done has set a foundation for monitoring and continually adapting as needed. You have built sets of analyses. You have established frameworks that need now only be maintained, as opposed to (re)building whole components of your entire organization. You have created a discipline and a rigor behind the work you do as a leader and team to ensure that the stage is set for remarkability. Your culture and your team are remarkable. Now, it will be a matter of polishing things up from time to time.

Staying remarkable is a practice that doesn't end, and below is a structure you can use to help keep the shine indefinitely.

The SAM Model for Staying Remarkable

If you have put in all the work to get to remarkability, you will want to make sure you stay there. The iterative process model below—the SAM model—offers a simple yet effective way to maintain remarkability status.

1. <u>Survey</u> the changing world around you, your customers, stakeholders, and the ways in which your organization is performing. Convene a diversity of perspectives and ideas. Hold strategic discussions as to needs, challenges, adaptation, evolution, and options.

2. <u>Adapt,</u> based on the findings of Survey, any element of your remarkable organization that is at risk of challenge or impairment.

3. <u>Measure</u> the impact of the adaptation that you put into place, evaluate the feedback, and make further adaptation if necessary.

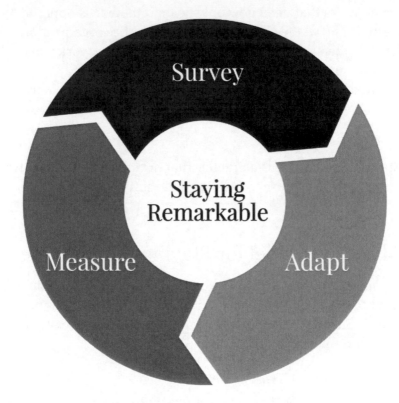

Below I break down each part of the model and illustrate them using an example of the Calgary Chamber's response to an economic recession in 2015.

Survey

Through the big picture analysis and financial assessment of your organization, you will have a robust means of continuing to evaluate your operational health. Through the Remarkability Agenda, you will have achieved a desired level of performance as compared to peers and historical performance. Continuing to evaluate your performance regularly (i.e., minimum once per year) in the same way will ensure that you stay where you want to be.

You should also regularly survey your customers and stakeholders—board, staff, members, etc.—to determine if you are achieving the levels and standards that you committed to through the remarkability journey. The market research and engagement approach discussed in Chapter 9 is something that should be done ideally twice per year, but once at minimum.

You will also continue the practice of assessing the world around you and the trends and forces that impact your organization's environment and performance. You should always be looking for and assessing things that will impact your purpose, people or platform. If you don't have the expertise or time, bring in people who are knowledgeable and can help to inform you of the potential impacts.

You also need to foster a culture of empowerment within your team such that ideas, suggestions and improvements to stay remarkable can come from any part or level of the organization. Often front-line staff who interact regularly with customers or members have the greatest sense of what works well and what does not. They often are the main users of your software or platforms and hear firsthand the feedback from the customers. You should create means and processes to enable that great insight and feedback to make its way to the right levels so that change or improvement investments can be made. While surveying customers is critical, so is tapping into the expertise and wisdom of staff. The same can be said of improvements internally, so continual staff engagement through regular surveys or other means can also ensure you remain remarkable as an employer.

Using the information gathered from the steps above, every 6-12 months bring together your leadership team and/or your board to engage in strategic conversations about maintaining remarkability. Maybe you don't need to change anything, or maybe you need to tune your value proposition or product and service mix. It will depend on what you find in your survey and what you decide to do with that information.

To illustrate the SAM model, let's use a situation that occurred in 2015 at the Calgary Chamber. At that time, the price of oil had been sliding down from a peak of around $100 per barrel in the spring of 2014. By the fall 2014, it had dropped down to below $30 per barrel. For Calgary, a city that relies heavily on the oil and gas sector, this plummet resulted in tens of thousands of people being laid off, the downtown office vacancy rate rising to 30%, bankruptcies, and business closures. It was a terrible time and one that called for an extraordinary response by the Calgary Chamber.

I spent many sleepless nights trying to think of what to do. Our community was wringing its hands and worrying about the future. People in the business community were desperate for some way to turn the situation around.

However, despite offering a variety of business programs, we had no program or service that could truly help people who had just lost 50% of their clients and revenue in the span of a few months. We had no program or service to help people find new customers or markets quickly. So, we surveyed our members and stakeholders as to the most meaningful response and support from the Chamber.

After discussing the results as a leadership team and a board, we concluded that we needed to develop a new program offering that could help people see the opportunities that lay ahead and help them pivot their business to find new applications, new customers and new markets.

We then embarked on an adaptation to our program and service offering in support of our members during a challenging economic time.

Adapt

Once you and your team have developed some options to consider, you may decide to make some adaptations in your value proposition or program and service offering. You should reflect on all three pillars of remarkability and each of their elements as possible areas of adaptation. The change and disruption that you may face could come from any side of the operation, or even multiple sides.

Based on the outcome of your survey and discussions, and assuming that there is some needed change, develop a pilot program or service to make sure that it is something that is well received and hits the mark. Again, this can be done internally, with a consultant, or harnessing the ideas of your target market or community. As articulated in Chapter 9, build something basic (a minimum viable product) and launch to see how it performs and is received by your target market. The next phase of the SAM model—measure—will enable you to assess how it is performing and adjust as needed.

These adaptations may be small, or they may be significant. Regardless, the approval process laid out in Chapter 4 will be a great approach to use for any further change proposal that you need to put in front of colleagues or your board of directors if a funding or major change ask is required. The processes and structures you used to get you to remarkability have application for further adaptation of the organization.

To flesh out the Calgary Chamber example above, our response to the desperation of our community led us to create a two-pronged initiative, a one-day innovation conference called the ONWARD Summit plus a 90-day innovation accelerator program called Ignite.

We needed an infusion of funding to support this program, and we didn't have the time to attempt to sponsor it—so we built a change proposal and funding request along the lines of the one from Chapter 4. We presented the pilot to the board for approval and were granted an initial wave of funds. We launched the ONWARD Summit conference to much success within three months (it is now the second largest annual event held by the Calgary Chamber) and got the first cohort of entrepreneurs into our Ignite accelerator within six months. The program is still going strong and is touted as one of Canada's most unique innovation programs for second stage companies. ONWARD and Ignite were both built quickly, using a lean start-up approach, knowing that we would be able to change and iterate over time, and that the first version would not be perfect.

Measure

Once the adaptation is launched, it is important to ensure that it is performing as desired. Measuring may include looking at the financial performance of your change or engaging with test subjects or stakeholders and asking for feedback on how to improve. Their experience with the new program or service will yield valuable feedback for you to adjust and further adapt (it may take multiple iterations and adaptations) until you find a version that makes sense and people are happy with.

Continuing the Calgary Chamber example, after we launched the Ignite innovation accelerator, we asked the first cohort of participants for feedback. They had some excellent input as to how to improve the experience and the process to achieve a greater outcome. We worked as a team to make the changes to the curriculum and program delivery for the second cohort. These changes made the program even better, but again we asked the second cohort participants for feedback on how to improve and they came back with a few suggestions. We made changes again to the curriculum for the third cohort and implemented that. Again, we asked for feedback and each time the list of things to change and improve got smaller, so we knew that we were heading in the right directions.

Through this cycle, the Calgary Chamber adapted, implemented and created value, all in a relatively short period of time and with minimal resources. We needed to stay remarkable and therefore built a process and culture of continually surveying, adapting and measuring. Once you get to where you want to be, you want to make sure that none of that hard work goes to waste.

Stay Remarkable: Never Take Your Eyes Off the Road

As mentioned at the beginning of *Making Remarkable*, the focus and commitment to remarkability demonstrated by an organization's CEO or leader establishes the standard and sets expectations for staff, board, members and stakeholders.

Once you have completed your Remarkability Agenda and you have got to a place you are happy with, implement the SAM model and make it part of your discipline and team process. It's likely that for the first while you won't need to make many, if any, adaptations. Your organization will be freshly remarkable and so there may be little change to make for a while.

You may find it useful to go through the diagnostic questions annually to see how you fare and to make sure you score 80% or better in each of the elements. Keeping fresh and current, and remarkable, is an ongoing practice. The SAM model is meant to help you do that.

If you want to stay remarkable, you must continue to set that tone and demonstrate that leadership. It can be tempting to take your eyes off the road if you reach a point when you feel you might ultimately be "there." I know. I know that temptation and have been guilty of losing focus from time to time.

Drifting attention from the road has a consequence. It's like with your muscles: if you keep lifting, they will remain strong—but take a break, and you lose some of that strength. Stay diligent and disciplined. Don't take your eyes off the road. Survey, adapt and measure. Always be thinking, looking, trying, testing, inspiring and delivering. Always. The benefits and rewards of remarkability are worth the effort.

Acknowledgements

Like all major efforts, I owe much to many. This book started as a seed of an idea from my wife Luiza. She encouraged me to put these ideas down. My friend and former colleague Scott Crockatt agreed. They both kept bugging me to write something. I am glad I did.

First to my family. To my children—Sofia, Thomas, Ana and Lucas—it is for you that I wish to leave a better world. Your patience and understanding, support and encouragement while I worked away on this book has reminded me that this work is for the long game. To my wife Luiza, your wisdom and insight into pretty much everything continues to amaze and inspire me. Thank you for the idea, support, encouragement and belief in me. The elements of this book on brand have been made richer and stronger because of your help. My heart and thanks to my beautiful family.

To my parents, you gave me the foundations from which to build a life and a career, and the drive to take on something as significant as writing a book—thank you for those gifts and for supporting my paths and my choices. To my sister, I admire everything you do, everyday—if there is a real-life Superwoman, it is you.

To my extended family, including my Brazilian family, you have always showed keen interest and enthusiasm, never wavering in your belief in me, and kindness in wanting to be the first to buy a copy. I am fortunate and grateful.

To my colleagues at the Calgary Chamber with whom I had the most amazing seven years and built lasting and meaningful relationships—thank you for working alongside me on this journey. I particularly want to thank my Leadership Team colleagues with whom I spent many an hour working, laughing, reflecting and doing remarkable things with: Scott Crockatt, Emma Covenden, Rebecca Wood, Aaron Kroontje, Michael Andriescu, Zoe Addington, Kim Koss and Jackie McAtee. Thank you all.

To the members of the Calgary Chamber Board of Directors who first hired me, and the ones who kept me—thank you. You challenged me, pushed me and made me a better leader. Your wisdom, experience and thoughtful guidance brought us from struggling to remarkable. I am indebted to you for your unwavering support. Specifically, grand appreciation to my board chairs throughout the years for your friendship and and guidance: Simon Vincent, Glenn McNamara, Dave Sprague, Joe Lougheed, Leah Lawrence, Rob Hawley, Denis Painchaud and David Allen.

To my mentors and friends who have supported me throughout my career, thank you for always being there to give insight, experience and perspective: Earl Williams, Simon Vincent, Jim Dinning, Dave Bronconnier, Jamal Ramjohn, Bradley Chisholm, Ian Chisholm, George Mathew, Michelle Berg, Jim Dewald, Mac Van Wielingen, James Boettcher, Jim Button, Guy Huntingford, Mike Williams, Lois Mitchell, Michel Leblanc, Iain Black, Janet Riopel, Jan De Silva, Loren Remillard, Dave Angus, Roy Williams, Joe Roman, Rick Baker, Casey Steinbacher, Judy Fairburn, Ken Kristofferson, Ray DePaul, Kevin Gregor, Diane Francis, Geoff Best, Hamish Knox, Mark Blackwell, Mathew Stone, Matthew Heffernan, Michael Brown, Clark Grue, Tom Sampson, Nicole Olenick, Ross Glen, Peter Tertzakian, Doug Black, Robbie Babins-Wagner, Ron Mannix, Chima Nkemdirim, Joe Lougheed, the brothers McCreath, Todd Hirsch, Phil Roberts, and Mick Fleming. Apologies to those whom I have no doubt missed.

Thank you to Harrison Coerver for being the spark that got me thinking of new ideas and for his thoughtful and helpful guidance in the writing of this book. Thank you to Peter Diamandis and Salim Ismail for opening my eyes to possibility.

To my friends and colleagues who supported my work and graciously reviewed early versions of the book, thank you for making suggestions that have created a more meaningful finished product: Sheree Anne Kelly, Kyle Sexton, Jay Byers, Jay Chesshir, Tim Giuliani, Betty Nokes Capestany, Mark Eagan, Michelle Berg, Scott Crockatt, Emma Covenden and Jennifer Diakiw. Thank you for the encouragement, enthusiasm and honesty.

To my editor Lorraine Valestuk—you carefully worked to make my book seem coherent and like I have command of the language; thank you. Thank you to my designer Sara Swallow— your ability to turn words into imagery is amazing. Thank you to Jim Gibson and Kyle Sexton for their insight and guidance as authors who helped to shorten the learning curve for me.

Finally, thank you to the community of friends who form the chamber of commerce network globally; to all my Canadian Chamber of Commerce and Chamber of Commerce Executives of Canada friends and colleagues—particularly for the privilege of serving as Canada's representative on the World Chamber Federation. Thank you to my ACCE friends and colleagues and my World Chamber Federation colleagues. It is a privilege to work with you and I am grateful for our collective efforts to make the world a better place.

Onward.

About the Author

Adam Legge works with executives, leaders and boards to help them achieve remarkability through organizational renewal and transformation. He believes in the potential of leaders to make their organizations remarkable and do work that can change their communities and the world.

When not helping clients become remarkable, Adam is also a Director at the Canadian Centre for Advanced Leadership in the Haskayne School of Business at the University of Calgary. Prior to his current roles, Adam was the 18th President and CEO of the Calgary Chamber of Commerce.

Adam lives with his family in Calgary, Alberta.

You can learn more about Adam and his work, services and speaking at www.adamlegge.com and www.makingremarkable.com

End Notes

1 https://en.wikiquote.org/wiki/Eric_Shinseki

2 The Remarkability Diagnostic questions and online tool are provided in good faith and not intended to replace a professional assessment of the needs of your organization. The tool and responses are not a substitute for professional advice and should not be used alone as a basis of decision or action.

3 Salim Ismail, *Exponential Organizations: Why new organizations are ten times better, faster, and cheaper than yours (and what to do about it).* Diversion Books (2014), p.42

4 http://startupquotes.startupvitamins.com/post/77385350314/your-brand-is-what-other-people-say-about-you

5 https://www.ted.com/talks/simon_sinek_how_great_leaders_inspire_action

6 Simon Sinek, *Find your Why: A Practical Guide for Discovering Purpose For You and Your Team.* Portfolio Penguin (2017). p. 30

7 The Remarkability Diagnostic questions and online tool are provided in good faith and not intended to replace a professional assessment of the needs of your organization. The tool and responses are not a substitute for professional advice and should not be used alone as a basis of decision or action.

8 https://www.forbes.com/sites/andrewcave/2017/11/09/culture-eats-strategy-for-breakfast-so-whats-for-lunch/#45fed6a77e0f

9 https://www.jimcollins.com/article_topics/articles/aligning-action.html

10 https://www.jimcollins.com/article_topics/articles/aligning-action.html

11 http://www.viewpointgroup.ca/public/images/Part_1_-_Governance_Strategy_and_the_Imperative_of_Performance.pdf

12 http://www.viewpointgroup.ca/public/images/Part_2_-_Culture_as_Governance_and_the_Link_with_Performance_-_Mac_Van_Wielingen_-_2017_(002).pdf

13 Simon Sinek, *Find your Why: A Practical Guide for Discovering Purpose For You and Your Team.* Portfolio Penguin (2017).

14 Alexander Osterwalder and Yves Pigneur, *Business Model Generation.* John Wiley and Sons Inc. (2010).

15 Jeffrey Krames, *Inside Drucker's Brain*, Gildan Media. (2011).

16 http://quotes.yourdictionary.com/articles/who-said-hope-is-not-strategy.html

[17] Salim Ismail, *Exponential Organizations: Why new organizations are ten times better, faster, and cheaper than yours (and what to do about it)*. Diversion Books (2014), p.130

[18] Salim Ismail, *Exponential Organizations: Why new organizations are ten times better, faster, and cheaper than yours (and what to do about it)*. Diversion Books (2014), p.93

[19] Ibid

[20] https://www.nytimes.com/2013/02/24/opinion/sunday/dowd-pompom-girl-for-feminism.html?ref=todayspaper&_r=3&

[21] Referencing the name of Alphabet's department and business line that tackles moonshots and large scale transformational projects, formerly known as Google X.

[22] TriStar Pictures